The Forex Strategist

Advanced Techniques for Market Dominance

By

Nathan Venture, D

To you,

Thank you!

Table of Contents

Introduction

Welcome to a journey through the intricate world of Forex trading. If you're holding this book, it's likely you've already dipped your toes into the vigorous currents of currency trading and are now looking to refine your skills. Maybe you've tasted both the sweetness of victory and the bitterness of losses. Either way, you're on the path to evolving from an intermediate trader to a more advanced, strategic player in the Forex market.

The Forex market is fascinating and complex, akin to a living organism that responds, adapts, and evolves based on a multitude of factors. It's a 24/5 marketplace that never sleeps, driven by economic forces, political events, and the endless push and pull of supply and demand. Mastery in this domain requires not only knowledge but also a keen sense of timing and psychological fortitude. Throughout this book, our goal is to help you deepen your understanding and proficiency, enabling you to navigate the treacherous waters of Forex trading with confidence and skill.

What sets successful traders apart isn't merely luck or intuition; it's a robust fusion of technical prowess, strategic planning, and mental resilience. The essence of Forex trading lies in understanding the market's underlying mechanics, developing tailored strategies, and maintaining discipline. This introduction serves as a prologue to an extensive exploration of topics that will equip you with advanced techniques and insights.

Throughout this book, each chapter has been meticulously crafted to build on your existing knowledge and introduce more sophisticated concepts. Whether it's technical analysis, risk management, or developing a strong trading mindset, we've pieced together a comprehensive guide that unfolds layer by layer.

We begin our journey with an understanding of the foundational elements of Forex trading. Chapter 1 will delve into the essentials—what moves the market, key economic indicators, and the critical importance of understanding these elements. Think of this as grounding yourself before scaling the heights of advanced strategies. You can't build a skyscraper on a shaky foundation, right?

Chapter 2 will help you set the stage for strategic success. It's vital to align your trading goals and identify the style that best suits you. Are you a day trader, or does swing trading resonate more with your schedule and risk appetite? This chapter emphasizes the role of discipline and consistency in crafting a robust trading strategy.

As we progress, we dive into the intricacies of technical analysis. Chapter 3 is all about mastering technical tools—understanding chart patterns, trend analysis, and the nuances that can often be the difference between a successful trade and a missed opportunity. Visualizing the market through various types of charts and patterns gives you the foresight needed to anticipate and act on market movements.

For those of you who rely on indicators, Chapter 4 enhances your understanding of leading versus lagging indicators and how to use them in conjunction with other tools. Indicators can provide vital clues about market momentum and potential reversals, but knowing how to use them effectively is where the magic happens.

Price action trading, a critical skill for advanced traders, takes center stage in Chapter 5. Here, you'll learn to interpret market behavior without the clutter of indicators, focusing solely on price movements. Strategies such as Pin Bar, Inside Bar, and Engulfing Patterns will be unraveled for you to incorporate into your trading arsenal.

Next, we address a crucial yet often overlooked aspect of trading: risk management. Chapter 6 lays out methods to understand and manage leverage, how to appropriately set stop losses and take profits, and the paramount importance of sizing your positions correctly. Effective risk management is the bedrock of sustainable trading success.

No trader can excel without mastering their psychology. Chapter 7 aims to address the mental aspects of trading—overcoming emotional pitfalls, nurturing patience, building confidence, and cultivating a resilient mindset. Trading isn't just a battle against the market; it's a battle against yourself, and winning that internal battle is half the victory.

Creating a robust trading plan is the focus of Chapter 8. A comprehensive plan that outlines your objectives, rules for entries and exits, and a mechanism for regular review can elevate your trading tactics. Successful trading is systematic and methodical, not random and impulsive.

In Chapter 9, we transition to the realm of algorithmic trading, illuminating how automated systems can be an asset in your trading toolbox. Whether you're looking to build your algorithms or understand the pros and cons of automated trading, this chapter offers a thorough introduction.

Advanced trading strategies get their due attention in Chapter 10, detailing the mechanics of scalping, day trading, swing trading, and the carry trade strategy. Each approach has its merits and challenges, and understanding these can help refine your approach.

Divergence trading, a nuanced technique that can provide powerful trading signals, is explored in Chapter 11. Understanding how to identify and trade divergences, and how to combine them with other strategies, can add a significant edge to your trading skill set.

Finally, the global impact on Forex trading is tackled in Chapter 12. Geopolitical events, currency correlations, and the influence of emerging markets are integral to understanding and anticipating market movements. Being well-versed in these areas allows you to make more informed decisions, especially in a market as globally intertwined as Forex.

This book aims to be your guide, mentor, and reference as you navigate the sophisticated and rewarding world of Forex trading. Each chapter builds upon the last, equipping you with the tools, strategies, and mindset necessary for consistent profitability. Let's embark on this journey to transform your trading approach, enhance your skillset, and ultimately, achieve your trading goals.

Are you ready to refine and elevate your trading game? Let's dive into the exciting world of Forex Trading!

Chapter 1: The Foundation of Forex Trading

Understanding the nuts and bolts of the Forex market lays the groundwork needed for effective trading. This arena, where global currencies are exchanged, operates around the clock, presenting both opportunities and challenges for traders. Knowledge of key factors that influence Forex prices, such as geopolitical events, interest rates, and economic indicators, is indispensable. Economic calendars become your best ally, flagging vital data releases that can sway market sentiment. A firm grasp of these fundamentals allows a trader to interpret market movements more accurately, setting the stage for more sophisticated trading strategies. Whether it's reading GDP reports or analyzing market demand and supply, mastering these elements ensures you're not just reacting to the market but anticipating it, setting the course for success in the intricate world of Forex trading.

Understanding the Forex Market

To truly thrive in the Forex market, it's crucial to understand the fundamentals that drive it. The Forex market, also known as the foreign exchange market, is a global decentralized market where currencies are traded. Unlike stock markets that operate from centralized exchanges, Forex operates 24 hours a day, five days a week, across various financial centers worldwide. This constant trading window offers opportunities and challenges that demand a deeper comprehension of market dynamics.

First, let's delve into what makes Forex unique. At its core, trading in the Forex market means buying one currency while simultaneously selling another. This pair-based structure is fundamental to understanding how trading decisions and strategies are developed. For example, if you believe the Euro will strengthen against the US Dollar, you might buy the EUR/USD currency pair. Conversely, if you think the US Dollar will strengthen, you would sell the pair.

The sheer volume and liquidity of the Forex market are other distinguishing features. With a daily trading volume exceeding $6 trillion, it stands as the largest financial market globally. High liquidity facilitates easier transactions and tighter spreads, making it an appealing playground for traders. Liquidity varies throughout the trading day, peaking during the overlap of major trading sessions such as London and New York.

Understanding market participants is pivotal. Central banks, financial institutions, hedge funds, corporations, and individual retail traders all converge in the Forex market. Central banks, like the Federal Reserve or the European Central Bank, can impact market sentiment and currency values through monetary policies and interventions. Financial institutions engage in Forex for speculative purposes and to balance their portfolios, while corporations might participate to hedge against currency risks associated with international trade.

One cannot overlook the influence of economic indicators on Forex prices. Variables such as interest rates, inflation data, GDP growth, employment reports, and consumer confidence indexes significantly affect currency valuations. For instance, if the Federal Reserve raises interest rates, it typically strengthens the US Dollar as investors seek higher returns. Conversely, disappointing GDP figures could weaken a currency as it reflects economic instability.

Geopolitical events and global developments can also swing Forex markets. Elections, natural disasters, trade agreements, or military conflicts introduce volatility and can lead to abrupt shifts in currency values. A savvy trader must stay abreast of global news and be ready to adjust strategies in response to geopolitical shifts. For instance, Brexit had a lasting impact on the British Pound, creating opportunities and risks for traders.

The concept of currency pairs opens a door to understanding the relative strength of different economies. Major pairs, like EUR/USD or GBP/USD, involve the most traded currencies and generally exhibit lower volatility due to their higher liquidity. Cross-currency pairs, excluding the USD, and exotic pairs from emerging markets offer high-risk, high-reward scenarios. The choice of pairs to trade can be influenced by factors like trading style, risk tolerance, and market familiarity.

Market sentiment, another subtle yet potent force, often dictates trading behavior. Sentiment analysis involves gauging the overall mood of investors—are they risk-averse or inclined towards risk-taking? Positive sentiment can propel currencies tied to economic growth, whereas a flight to safety might boost traditionally safe-haven currencies like the Swiss Franc or Japanese Yen.

Then there's the realm of technical analysis, an indispensable tool for Forex traders. Price charts, candlestick patterns, and technical indicators all serve to identify trends, potential breakout points, and market reversals. Past price movements are scrutinized to forecast future performance. Mastery of technical analysis helps in making informed decisions, enhancing the probability of successful trades.

Another essential aspect is understanding market mechanisms such as spreads, pips, and lot sizes. The spread—the difference between the bid and ask price—affects trading costs. Pips measure the smallest price movement in a currency pair, crucial for calculating potential profits or losses. Lot sizes determine the trade volume, with standard, mini, and micro lots offering flexibility based on account size and risk appetite.

In essence, grasping the Forex market's intricacies involves a blend of strategic thinking, constant education, and adaptability. Markets evolve, influenced by myriad factors ranging from economic indicators and geopolitical events to technological advancements in trading platforms. Staying ahead requires not only understanding current fundamentals but also anticipating future market shifts. Experience, coupled with a robust analytical approach, can transform volatility from a challenge into an opportunity.

To encapsulate, the Forex market's complexity should not deter but rather excite the dedicated trader. Knowing its structure, participants, and influencing factors lays a foundation upon which sophisticated strategies can be built. Whether it's deciphering economic indicators or mastering technical analysis, a comprehensive understanding of the Forex market equips traders to navigate it with greater skill and confidence. This journey of continuous learning and strategic application is what sets the successful apart in the dynamic world of Forex trading.

Key Factors Influencing Forex Prices

Understanding the key factors influencing Forex prices is essential for traders aiming to refine their skills and improve profitability. At its core, Forex trading revolves around the relative strength of one currency against another. This dynamic interplay is driven by a myriad of factors that can shift the balance, creating opportunities—or pitfalls—for traders. Knowing what moves the market enables you to anticipate changes, align your strategies, and make informed trading decisions.

At the macroeconomic level, **interest rates** are one of the most influential factors affecting Forex prices. Central banks use interest rates as a tool to control inflation and stabilize their country's currency. Generally, higher interest rates offer lenders in an economy a better return relative to other countries. Consequently, currencies from countries with higher interest rates attract more capital investment, driving up their value. It's not just the interest rate level that matters, but also changes in interest rate expectations. Traders often try to predict these changes by closely monitoring central bank meetings and economic reports.

The role of **inflation** in influencing Forex prices cannot be overstated. Inflation represents the rate at which the general level of prices for goods and services is rising. When inflation is high, the purchasing power of a currency is eroded. Central banks may raise interest rates to combat inflation, but if inflation is much higher than other countries, the currency might depreciate even with increasing interest rates. Thus, understanding the current inflation environment and predicting future trends is crucial for any serious Forex trader.

Economic indicators serve as a pulse check on the health of an economy. GDP growth rates, employment data, and manufacturing outputs are some of the primary indicators traders use to gauge economic strength. A strong economy tends to attract foreign investment, increasing the demand for the local currency and pushing its value higher. Conversely, weak economic performance can lead to currency devaluation. Economic indicators release on a fixed schedule, allowing traders to prepare for and react to these critical data points.

Moving beyond fundamental factors, **geopolitical events** can significantly influence Forex prices, often creating sharp and unpredictable market movements. Election results, political instability, trade negotiations, and international conflicts can induce rapid currency fluctuations. For example, election outcomes can shape economic policies, and the anticipation of these changes often creates volatility in currency markets. Understanding the geopolitical landscape and staying updated with news developments is indispensable for navigating these turbulent waters.

Another layer of complexity is added by **market sentiment** and trader psychology. Forex markets, like all financial markets, are influenced by the collective psychology of its participants. Expectations, fears, and predictions drive decision-making processes, fueling trends, and reversals. Market sentiment can be influenced by a variety of factors, including news events, economic reports, and even social media. Gauging sentiment can be challenging, but tools like the Commitment of Traders (COT) reports and sentiment indices can provide valuable insights.

Currency **correlations** also play a pivotal role in Forex trading. Some currencies tend to move in the same direction, while others move inversely. Understanding these relationships can help you predict and hedge against future price movements. For instance, the positive correlation between the Australian dollar and gold prices means that if gold prices rise, the Australian dollar is likely to strengthen. Recognizing these patterns and understanding the reasons behind them allow traders to make more holistic trading decisions.

While economic theories provide a foundational understanding, **speculation** and market liquidity add a speculative layer. Forex markets are highly liquid, meaning currencies can be quickly bought or sold with minimal price changes. However, this liquidity also attracts speculators looking to profit from short-term movements. Speculative trades can amplify movements caused by fundamental factors. You'll often observe sharp price movements during major economic releases, driven by the actions of speculators positioning themselves ahead of or reacting to the news.

Another interesting factor is the influence of **social and cultural factors**, though less direct. For instance, trading habits and practices vary across regions. During periods of increased tourism, the demand for certain currencies can rise, impacting exchange rates. Festivals, holidays, and tourism seasons often see significant swings that can spell opportunities or risks for the aware trader.

Lastly, **technological advancements** and algorithmic trading have reshaped the Forex landscape. Modern trading platforms provide real-time data and advanced charting tools that are indispensable for analysis. Algorithmic trading systems can process enormous amounts of data and execute trades at lightning speed. As more traders and funds employ these technologies, their influence on price movements has grown, creating both opportunities and challenges for human traders. The key here is not just understanding the technology but also monitoring how it shapes market dynamics.

Summing up, mastering the key factors influencing Forex prices involves a multifaceted approach. You must blend an understanding of economic fundamentals, geopolitical events, market sentiment, correlations, and the latest technological tools. Each factor alone holds predictive power, but it's the interplay between them that often determines market direction. With a strong grasp of these elements, you can elevate your trading strategies and position yourself for greater success in the Forex market.

The Importance of Economic Indicators

In the realm of Forex trading, economic indicators are essential to making informed decisions. For intermediate and advanced traders, understanding these indicators isn't just optional; it's crucial for refining strategies and increasing profitability. Let's dive into why these indicators are so impactful.

Economic indicators act as the pulse of an economy. They provide critical insights into a country's economic health and influence currency movements. By monitoring these indicators, traders can anticipate shifts in market sentiment and adjust their positions accordingly. For instance, a higher-than-expected GDP growth rate often results in a stronger currency, while disappointing employment figures might lead a currency to depreciate.

Consider indicators like GDP (Gross Domestic Product), unemployment rates, and inflation. GDP measures the economic output and growth of an economy. A robust GDP growth suggests a strong economy, attracting foreign investment and increasing demand for that nation's currency. Unemployment rates, on the other hand, reflect the health of the labor market. High unemployment often signifies economic distress, leading to weaker currency performance.

Inflation is another critical factor. It measures the rate at which the general level of prices for goods and services rises, eroding purchasing power. Central banks closely monitor inflation and adjust interest rates to keep it under control. If inflation is rising too quickly, a central bank might hike interest rates to slow it down. This increase in interest rates can make a country's currency more attractive to investors seeking higher returns, thus strengthening it.

Interest rates themselves are a pivotal indicator. The policies set forth by central banks (e.g., the Federal Reserve, European Central Bank) profoundly impact currency valuation. When a central bank raises interest rates, it often strengthens the national currency because higher interest rates offer better returns on investments denominated in that currency. Conversely, lowering interest rates can weaken the currency due to reduced investment appeal.

Trade balance and current account data are also significant. A trade surplus (when exports exceed imports) usually strengthens a currency because it represents higher foreign demand. Conversely, a trade deficit might weaken the currency as it indicates more imports than exports, increasing foreign currency demand to pay for these imports.

Let's not overlook the importance of consumer and business sentiment indices. Indicators like the Consumer Confidence Index (CCI) and Purchasing Managers' Index (PMI) provide insight into the mood of consumers and businesses. High confidence usually parallels spending and investment, leading to economic growth and potentially strengthening the currency. Low confidence, however, can signal economic slowdowns and consequently weaken the currency.

One of the most critical releases that traders watch closely are employment figures, especially the Non-Farm Payroll (NFP) report in the United States. The NFP shows the number of jobs added or lost outside the farming sector and significantly impacts the USD. Strong employment growth can signal a healthy economy, leading to currency appreciation. Poor employment growth, however, can spur economic pessimism and drive the currency lower.

Economic indicators don't just offer insights into the health of a country's economy. They also impact market expectations and central bank policy moves. Traders often try to anticipate these policy moves to position themselves advantageously. For example, if inflation data indicates it's rising faster than expected, traders might expect the central bank to raise interest rates sooner rather than later, prompting them to buy the currency in anticipation of future gains.

Geopolitical events and natural disasters can disrupt economic stability, rendering traditional indicators less predictive in the short term. During such times, traders might lean on economic indicators to gauge the resilience and recovery pace of the affected economy. Conversely, stable periods make these indicators more reliable for predictive modeling and strategy formulation.

Additionally, economic indicators are part of fundamental analysis, which complements technical analysis. While technical analysis focuses on past price movements to predict future trends, fundamental analysis delves into economic indicators, financial metrics, and central bank policies. Combining both approaches provides traders with a more comprehensive view of market conditions and enhances decision-making.

Economic calendars are invaluable tools for Forex traders. These calendars list dates and times for the release of major economic indicators, along with previous and expected values. By keeping an eye on these releases, traders can prepare for increased market volatility and plan their trades accordingly. Utilizing economic calendars, traders can reduce the element of surprise and manage risk more effectively.

Let's delve into how traders can integrate economic indicators into their trading strategies. One common approach is event-driven trading, where traders open positions based on anticipated economic releases. For example, if a trader expects a strong GDP report, they might buy the currency ahead of the release. Conversely, if they anticipate disappointing employment data, they might sell.

Back-testing strategies that incorporate economic indicators is also prudent. Traders can look at how past economic releases impacted currency pairs and use this data to refine their strategies. Back-testing helps validate the reliability of indicators and aligns them with the trader's risk tolerance and objectives.

Risk management cannot be overstated when trading based on economic indicators. Market reactions to economic releases can be swift and unpredictable. Employing stop-loss orders and position sizing techniques ensures that potential losses remain within acceptable levels. Effective risk management allows traders to capitalize on opportunities while safeguarding their capital.

Lastly, staying updated with global economic trends and news can't be ignored. Economic indicators explain the "what" and "why" behind market movements, but traders need constant information flow to interpret these correctly. Subscribing to market news services, following economic blogs, and maintaining an active role in trading communities enhance a trader's ability to react and adapt quickly.

In conclusion, economic indicators are the bedrock of informed Forex trading, especially for intermediate and advanced traders aiming to fine-tune their strategies. These indicators offer vital insights into a country's economic performance, influencing market sentiment and central bank policies. By staying attuned to these signals, integrating them into trading strategies, and managing associated risks, traders can significantly improve their chances of success in the dynamic Forex market.

Chapter 2: Crafting Your Forex Trading Strategy

Building a robust Forex trading strategy is the cornerstone of becoming a successful trader. It's about setting clear trading goals and aligning them with a style that suits your personality and lifestyle. Whether you favor day trading, position trading, or scalping, defining your approach and sticking to it with discipline is crucial. Consistency isn't just a buzzword; it's the bedrock upon which profitable trading is built. Seasoned traders know that the market doesn't reward haphazard decisions. Instead, having a well-thought-out strategy backed by both technical and fundamental analysis allows you to navigate the market's complexities with confidence. As you refine your strategy, remember: adaptation and continuous learning are key to staying ahead in the ever-evolving forex landscape.

Defining Your Trading Goals

Before you can set out on any journey, you need a clear understanding of where you want to go. Crafting an effective forex trading strategy begins with defining your trading goals. This chapter aims to help you crystallize your objectives, laying the foundation for strategies that can help you achieve those targets.

Your trading goals form the bedrock of your entire trading plan. Think of them as a roadmap guiding you through the forex market. They offer a sense of direction, keeping you focused amid the ups and downs of trading. Vague aspirations like "I want to make money" won't cut it. You need specific, measurable, attainable, relevant, and time-bound (SMART) goals to guide your trading activities.

Consider breaking down your goals into short-term and long-term objectives. Short-term goals could be related to daily or weekly performance metrics—like improving your win rate by a certain percentage or sticking to your trading plan without deviation for a month. Long-term goals might encompass achieving a specific return on investment (ROI) annually or growing your trading account to a predetermined size. Having a mixture of both helps you stay grounded and focused on different horizons.

The next step in defining your trading goals involves a deep introspection of your financial situation. Assess your current financial status, risk tolerance, and capital allocation. How much can you afford to lose? Understanding your risk tolerance is critical because it aligns your goals with your emotional capacity to manage losses. Not aligning your goals with your risk tolerance can lead to stress, poor decision-making, and ultimately, financial ruin.

When setting your goals, consider the style of trading that best suits you. Are you looking to day trade, scalp, or perhaps swing trade? Each trading style comes with its own set of strategies, risks, and rewards. Day trading might require you to set goals around capturing daily price movements, while swing trading could focus on capitalizing on medium-term trends. Tailor your goals accordingly.

Consistency and discipline are crucial when it comes to goal achievement. Once your goals are defined, the next logical step is embedding them into your daily trading routine. This could mean maintaining a trading journal to track your progress, analyzing your trades regularly, and making necessary adjustments to stay aligned with your objectives. Inconsistencies between your goals and your trading behaviors can derail even the most sophisticated strategies.

It's also important to continually review and reassess your goals. Markets evolve, personal circumstances change, and what might have been a relevant goal six months ago might need tweaking today. Regular check-ins—quarterly or bi-annually—ensure that your goals remain relevant and attainable. This adaptive approach prevents you from becoming too rigid, which can stifle your trading progress.

Don't underestimate the role of emotional and psychological objectives in your goal-setting process. Think about the kind of trader you aspire to be: Do you want to be known for your patience, your ability to stay calm under pressure, or perhaps your meticulous approach to analysis? Incorporating these qualitative aspects into your goal-setting framework can help you develop a more rounded and adaptable trading persona.

Of course, achieving your goals isn't just about discipline and strategy; it also involves continuous learning and adaptation. The forex market is dynamic, influenced by myriad factors ranging from economic indicators to geopolitical events. Thus, part of your goal-setting process should include milestones related to education—like completing advanced trading courses, obtaining relevant certifications, or mastering new trading tools and platforms.

Furthermore, your goals should be aligned with a clear understanding of your trading strengths and weaknesses. Conduct a SWOT analysis (Strengths, Weaknesses, Opportunities, Threats) to gain insights into areas where you excel and where you need improvement. Design your goals to leverage your strengths and mitigate your weaknesses. For instance, if emotional trading is a weakness, your goal might be to develop and stick to a stringent trading psychology plan.

Lastly, financial goals should translate into actionable trading strategies and tactics. For example, if your goal is to achieve a 10% ROI annually, break that down into monthly or even weekly targets. Then, define the specific trading tactics that will help you achieve those targets. Do you need to adopt a more aggressive trading style? Or perhaps, fine-tune your risk management techniques? Every financial goal should have a corresponding set of actions, making the journey toward achieving them more structured and realistic.

In conclusion, setting well-defined trading goals is a critical step in crafting an effective forex trading strategy. These goals provide the clarity and direction needed to navigate the complexities of the forex market. Whether your aspirations are financial, psychological, or educational, structuring them within a SMART framework greatly enhances your chances of success. Consistent with these aspirations, you'll be better equipped to develop trading strategies that are not only sophisticated and effective but also deeply aligned with your personal trading philosophy and risk tolerance. So take the time to define your goals meticulously; it might just be the most crucial investment you make in your trading journey.

Selecting the Right Trading Style

Choosing the right trading style is a crucial step in crafting your forex trading strategy. Your trading style not only influences your approach to the market but also determines the tools and techniques you'll use. It's essential to select a style that aligns with your personality, lifestyle, and trading goals. Each trading style has its own advantages and disadvantages, and finding the right fit can significantly impact your success as a forex trader.

There are several trading styles to consider, each with unique characteristics and requirements. Broadly speaking, forex traders can be classified into four primary categories: scalpers, day traders, swing traders, and position traders. Understanding the nuances of each style will help you make an informed decision about which one suits you best.

1. **Scalping**

Scalping is a high-frequency trading style that involves making numerous trades to capture small price movements. Scalpers often hold positions for just a few seconds to a few minutes, aiming to profit from tiny price fluctuations that occur within very short time frames. This style requires a high level of concentration, quick decision-making, and an in-depth understanding of market conditions.

Scalpers thrive on high liquidity and volatility, often targeting major currency pairs that offer tight spreads. The key to successful scalping lies in minimizing transaction costs and maximizing execution speed. Scalping demands a significant time commitment and a strong stomach for stress, as the rapid pace of trading can be intense.

2. **Day Trading**

Day trading involves holding positions for a single trading day, with traders closing all their positions by the end of the day to avoid overnight risk. Day traders aim to profit from intraday price movements and typically make several trades throughout the day. This style requires a solid understanding of technical analysis, as well as the ability to react quickly to market developments.

Day traders often use a combination of chart patterns, technical indicators, and news events to make informed trading decisions. While day trading can be lucrative, it also requires considerable time, focus, and discipline. Additionally, the need to constantly monitor the markets can be mentally taxing, making it unsuitable for those who prefer a more relaxed approach.

3. **Swing Trading**

Swing trading is a medium-term trading style that involves holding positions for several days to a few weeks. Swing traders aim to profit from price swings or "waves" in the market, often relying on technical analysis and chart patterns to identify potential entry and exit points.

This style offers a balance between the fast-paced nature of day trading and the longer-term approach of position trading.

Swing traders typically use a combination of technical analysis and fundamental analysis to make trading decisions. They look for trends and patterns in price charts, as well as key economic indicators and news events that could impact the market. Swing trading requires patience and the ability to tolerate periods of market uncertainty, as trades may not always move in the trader's favor immediately.

4. Position Trading

Position trading is a long-term trading style that involves holding positions for weeks, months, or even years. Position traders aim to profit from major trends and fundamental shifts in the market, often utilizing a combination of technical and fundamental analysis to identify long-term opportunities.

This style is well-suited for traders who prefer a hands-off approach and are willing to endure short-term fluctuations in pursuit of larger gains. Position trading requires a deep understanding of macroeconomic factors and a strong conviction in one's analysis. It also demands patience and the ability to maintain a long-term perspective, even in the face of short-term volatility.

Selecting the right trading style is a personal decision that depends on various factors, including your risk tolerance, time availability, and trading objectives. Here are some considerations to help you determine which style might be the best fit for you:

- *Risk Tolerance:* Each trading style has a different risk profile. Scalping and day trading involve higher levels of risk due to frequent trades and shorter time frames, while swing and position trading typically entail lower risk but require more patience and a longer-term perspective.

- *Time Commitment:* Consider how much time you can dedicate to trading. Scalping and day trading demand constant attention and quick decision-making, while swing and position trading allow for more flexibility and less frequent monitoring.
- *Personality:* Your trading personality plays a significant role in choosing the right style. If you enjoy fast-paced environments and can handle stress well, scalping or day trading may be suitable. If you prefer a more relaxed approach and can remain patient, swing or position trading might be a better fit.
- *Experience Level:* Your level of experience and expertise in forex trading can also influence your choice. Beginners might find swing or position trading more manageable, while more experienced traders may be better equipped to handle the complexities of scalping or day trading.
- *Trading Goals:* Clearly define your trading goals and choose a style that aligns with them. If your goal is to generate consistent daily income, day trading might be appropriate. If you're looking to build wealth over time, swing or position trading could be more suitable.

Ultimately, there is no one-size-fits-all answer when it comes to selecting the right trading style. The key is to experiment with different styles, monitor your performance, and make adjustments based on your observations. As you gain experience and refine your skills, you'll develop a deeper understanding of which style best suits your unique needs and preferences.

Remember, the right trading style is the one that complements your strengths, fits your lifestyle, and enables you to achieve your trading goals with confidence and consistency. By selecting the right trading style, you're laying a solid foundation for your forex trading strategy and setting yourself up for long-term success in the market.

In the next section, we'll delve into the importance of discipline and consistency in trading, exploring how these attributes can enhance your strategy and boost your overall performance.

The Role of Discipline and Consistency

For experienced traders, the forex market presents a range of opportunities that can be incredibly rewarding. Yet, without discipline and consistency, even the most promising trading strategies can falter. Discipline and consistency form the bedrock of any successful trading operation. They ensure that your methods are not just theories but practical, sustainable practices.

Discipline in forex trading involves sticking to your trading plan, no matter the emotional pressures you may face. It might seem somewhat paradoxical. On the one hand, the forex market is incredibly dynamic; prices can change in the blink of an eye. On the other, adhering to a predefined strategy requires a level of rigidity. The key is to strike a balance; adapt to new data without deviating from your core strategy.

Consistency is equally crucial. In any trading strategy, you might have phases where the market seems to defy logic and your positions incur losses. However, a consistent approach allows for statistical validation over time. This means that your overall strategy needs to be tested across various market conditions to prove its efficacy. If you're constantly changing your methods, it becomes almost impossible to determine which elements are working and which are not.

In the realm of forex trading, discipline starts before you even place a trade. It involves the careful planning and vetting of potential trades. Do the technical indicators align with your broader market analysis? Are you trading in congruence with the economic calendar? Each of these questions must be answered affirmatively before proceeding.

Once a trade is entered, discipline manifests as adherence to your pre-established rules regarding stop losses and take-profit levels. These markers shouldn't be changed on a whim, even if the market appears to be moving favorably. By sticking to your stops and targets, you're ensuring that your emotions don't override your rational trading decisions. It's this level of rigor that separates successful traders from the rest.

Consistency, meanwhile, is observed through routine. Successful traders often have a strict schedule they follow. Market analysis, entry and exit from trades, and review of performance are all undertaken at regular intervals. This repeated behavior not only engrains good habits but also provides a large dataset to analyze, reaffirming what works and what doesn't in your strategy.

Backtesting is a powerful tool in ensuring your discipline and consistency are up to par. Historical data analysis allows you to see how your strategies would have performed under various market conditions. When done properly, backtesting can significantly boost your confidence, showing you where your methods shine and where they might need tweaking. It's an exercise of discipline to invest time in backtesting, but the long-term benefits are undeniable.

Beyond the discipline of maintaining your trading plan, another less spoken-about aspect of forex trading is the discipline required in continuing education. The forex market is a constantly evolving beast, influenced by countless variables, including geopolitical events, economic changes, and market sentiment. Staying updated with these changes and understanding their impacts on your strategy demands persistent learning and adaptation.

Developing discipline and consistency isn't devoid of challenges. Emotional trading is a common roadblock many traders face. Understanding your emotions, acknowledging them, and ensuring they don't interfere with your trading decisions is an exercise in emotional intelligence. Journaling can be a highly effective tool here. By documenting your trades and the emotions experienced through the process, patterns can be identified and addressed.

Consistency in education goes hand in hand with discipline in practice. One without the other can only take you so far. Continuous learning keeps your strategies robust and adaptable, while disciplined adherence to your plan ensures those strategies are executed effectively.

A practical method to develop discipline is setting strict rules for yourself and unwaveringly adhering to them. For instance, never risk more than a certain percentage of your account on a single trade, for example, 1%. By implementing such rules and committing to them, you are building the muscle of discipline. In the beginning, this might feel restrictive, but over time you'll realize it was for your benefit. This discipline helps in preserving your capital and putting you in a position to exploit market opportunities effectively.

Additionally, accountability can play a significant role in fostering discipline. Having a trading mentor or being part of a trading community where there is a ritual of sharing your trading plans and results can add an extra layer of accountability. Sharing your performance data not only helps gain insights from others but also makes you more committed to your trading discipline.

Consistency also means not jumping from one strategy to another based on short-term performance. It's tempting to abandon a strategy after a few losses and switch to another, thinking the grass might be greener there. However, such fluctuations indicate a lack of conviction and understanding of your strategy's long-term viability. Stick to a well-thought-out plan and allow it the time needed for results to manifest.

Remember, the forex market is a marathon, not a sprint. Sustainable success and profitability come to those who practice disciplined trading and maintain consistency. This means committing to a long-term vision and resisting the urge for impulsive, short-term actions. The role of discipline and consistency extends beyond mere trading practices to encompass one's overall approach to learning and adapting in the market.

In conclusion, while flashy indicators and complex strategies can add value, the core drivers of long-term success in forex trading are discipline and consistency. They form an invisible but crucial backbone that supports all your trading activities. By integrating these principles into your everyday trading routine, you're not just setting yourself up for individual trade success but for a lasting, profitable trading career. Becoming a disciplined and consistent trader is less about finding the perfect strategy and more about cultivating the right mindset and habits to deploy any strategy effectively.

Chapter 3: Technical Analysis Mastery

As we dive deeper into the world of technical analysis, it's crucial to grasp the significance of chart types and patterns, which form the backbone of any seasoned trader's toolkit. By mastering candlestick formations and classical chart patterns, you'll decode market sentiment and predict price movements with greater accuracy. Trend analysis, through the utilization of moving averages and the identification of support and resistance levels, allows traders to spot potential entry and exit points effectively. Combining these techniques, you create a nuanced perspective of market dynamics, enabling timely decision-making and enhancing your overall trading strategy. Remember, technical analysis isn't just about looking at charts; it's about interpreting what they reveal and leveraging that insight for profitable trades.

Chart Types and Patterns

Technical analysis is the cornerstone of Forex trading, and a comprehensive understanding of chart types and patterns is pivotal for refining your strategies and increasing profitability. In this section, we delve into the diverse types of charts, such as line charts, bar charts, and the ever-popular candlestick charts, which provide visual representations of price movements over specific periods. Recognizing and interpreting various chart patterns, including head and shoulders, double tops and bottoms, and triangles, allows traders to predict potential market movements and devise strategic entry and exit points.

Mastery of these chart types and patterns isn't just about identifying shapes or lines; it's about understanding market psychology and leveraging this knowledge to make informed trading decisions. This foundational grasp of charts and patterns is essential for anyone aiming to navigate the complexities of the Forex market with confidence and precision.

Candlestick Patterns are a cornerstone of technical analysis and provide a visual representation of price movements in the Forex market. While many different chart types exist, candlestick charts are favored among traders for their ability to offer detailed information about the market sentiment and potential future price action. By interpreting the formations and patterns of candlesticks, traders can make more informed decisions and develop sophisticated trading strategies.

Candlestick charts originated in Japan and were used by rice traders in the 18th century. Each candlestick represents the price action within a specific time frame, such as one minute, one hour, or one day. A single candlestick consists of a body and shadows, also known as wicks, which extend above and below the body. The body of the candlestick shows the opening and closing prices, while the shadows indicate the highest and lowest prices reached during that time frame.

One of the fundamental concepts to understand in **candlestick patterns** is the distinction between bullish and bearish formations. A bullish candlestick indicates that the closing price is higher than the opening price, suggesting upward momentum. In contrast, a bearish candlestick shows that the closing price is lower than the opening price, indicating downward momentum. Recognizing these formations allows traders to gauge market direction and potential reversals.

The **Doji** is a pivotal candlestick pattern that signifies indecision in the market. When a Doji forms, the opening and closing prices are virtually identical, resulting in a small body with long shadows. This pattern can indicate a potential reversal, especially after a strong trend. The placement of the Doji within the trend often determines its significance; for instance, a Doji at the top of an uptrend may suggest a bearish reversal.

Another critical pattern is the **Engulfing pattern**, which can be either bullish or bearish. A bullish engulfing pattern occurs when a small bearish candlestick is followed by a larger bullish candlestick that completely engulfs the previous candle's body. This pattern signals that buyers have taken control and an upward movement may be imminent. Conversely, a bearish engulfing pattern happens when a small bullish candlestick is followed by a larger bearish candlestick, indicating sellers are gaining dominance and a downward trend might follow.

Two other essential candlestick patterns to master are the **Hammer** and the **Shooting Star**. The Hammer forms at the bottom of a downtrend and features a small body with a long lower shadow, suggesting the market tested lower prices but rejected them, potentially signaling a bullish reversal. On the other hand, the Shooting Star appears at the top of an uptrend and has a small body with a long upper shadow. This pattern indicates that the market reached higher levels but failed to sustain them, hinting at a bearish reversal.

In addition to individual patterns, traders often look at **candlestick sequences** for more comprehensive insights. The **Morning Star** and **Evening Star** are prime examples. A Morning Star consists of three candles: a long bearish candlestick, a shorter candlestick (often a Doji), and a long bullish candlestick. This pattern indicates that the selling pressure is diminishing, and buyers are starting to take over. Conversely, an Evening Star is seen at the end of an uptrend and comprises a long bullish candlestick, a short candlestick, and a long bearish candlestick, suggesting a bearish reversal.

The **Three Black Crows** and **Three White Soldiers** are powerful reversal patterns that traders should also be acquainted with. Three Black Crows consist of three consecutive bearish candlesticks, each closing near the low of the day. This pattern often signals the end of an uptrend and the beginning of a downtrend. Conversely, Three White Soldiers include three consecutive bullish candlesticks, indicating a strong shift from bearish to bullish sentiment.

Beyond understanding specific patterns, it is crucial to consider the **context** within which patterns form. Market conditions, such as trends, support and resistance levels, and overall market sentiment, play a significant role in validating or questioning the reliability of candlestick patterns. For example, a Hammer at a significant support level holds more weight than one that forms in the middle of a range-bound market.

Another advanced consideration is the concept of **volume** accompanying candlestick patterns. Often, the effectiveness of a candlestick pattern is enhanced when there is significant trading volume. High volume during a bullish pattern, for example, validates the pattern as it shows strong buying interest. Similarly, a bearish pattern with high volume confirms selling interest. Integrating volume analysis with candlestick patterns can yield higher accuracy in predicting market behavior.

It's also essential to understand that no single candlestick pattern works in isolation. Successful traders often combine multiple patterns and other technical analysis tools, such as moving averages and indicators, to form a comprehensive trading strategy. For instance, a trader might use the Relative Strength Index (RSI) alongside candlestick patterns to confirm overbought or oversold conditions before placing a trade.

To become proficient in reading candlestick patterns, practice is indispensable. Analyzing historical data and practicing on demo accounts can help you familiarize yourself with various patterns and their outcomes in real-market scenarios. Over time, you can sharpen your skills, better interpret market sentiments, and enhance your trading decisions.

In conclusion, **candlestick patterns** offer a window into market psychology and can significantly enhance your technical analysis toolkit when used effectively. By mastering these patterns and incorporating them into a broader trading strategy, you can gain a deeper understanding of price movements and improve your trading performance. Consistent practice and continual learning will ensure that you stay ahead in the ever-evolving Forex market.

Classical Chart Patterns stand as vital components of the technical analyst's toolkit. They're graphical representations that depict historical price movements, helping traders anticipate future price behaviors. To leverage classical chart patterns effectively, you must understand both their formation and the underlying psychology driving them. Unlike candlestick patterns, which pinpoint specific price action, classical chart patterns often require a broader lens, covering days, weeks, or even months. This section will guide you through recognizing and applying some of the most critical classical chart patterns in Forex trading.

First up, we've got the quintessential **Head and Shoulders pattern**. This reversal pattern is recognized by its three peaks: a taller middle peak flanked by two shorter ones. The higher middle peak forms the "head," while the surrounding peaks are the "shoulders." The "neckline" connects the lowest points of the two troughs, situated between the shoulders and the head. The pattern suggests a trend reversal is imminent. When the price breaks below the neckline after forming the right shoulder, it's typically time to sell. For an inverse Head and Shoulders, it's the opposite: When the price breaks above the neckline after forming the right shoulder, it signals a buying opportunity.

The **Double Top and Double Bottom patterns** are next on the list. Both are reversal patterns signaling a change in the current trend direction. A Double Top, resembling the letter "M," forms after a noticeable uptrend and indicates a bearish reversal upon completion. The price hits a peak (first top), retraces, rebounds to a similar height (second top), and finally breaks below the initial retracement low. Conversely, a Double Bottom, looking like a "W," indicates a bullish reversal. It forms after a significant downtrend when the price makes two almost identical lows before breaking above the pivot high nestled between the troughs.

Let's delve into continuation patterns, starting with the **Triangle patterns**. These include ascending, descending, and symmetrical triangles. A *Symmetrical Triangle* suggests a state of equilibrium, depicted by two converging trendlines with equal slope. The breakout direction upon pattern completion often defines the subsequent trend. An *Ascending Triangle* has a flat upper trendline and ascending lower trendline, indicating bullish sentiment. Conversely, the *Descending Triangle* reveals bearish sentiment with a flat lower trendline and descending upper trendline. In all cases, a breakout often signals a strong move in the direction of the breakout.

The **Flag and Pennant patterns** are fantastic for traders dealing with sharp price movements followed by brief consolidation periods. A *Flag* resembles a small parallelogram that slopes against the prevailing trend. It's essentially a brief pause within a robust trend, and upon breaking out, the price generally continues in the direction of the initial sharp move. A *Pennant*, on the other hand, is similar but smaller and more triangular. Its sloping converging lines suggest a compression of volatility, which is usually followed by a sharp price move in the initial trend direction upon breakout. Both patterns are great for catching momentum and continuation.

The **Rectangle pattern** is another significant continuation formation. This pattern consists of a price series that oscillates between two parallel horizontal lines, forming a rectangular shape. The pattern suggests a period of consolidation before the price breaks out in the direction of the prior trend. If the rectangle forms after an uptrend, the breakout is more likely to the upside, and conversely, if after a downtrend, a downward breakout is expected. The longer the duration of the rectangle, the more significant the breakout tends to be, as prolonged consolidation accumulates trading interest and energy.

We can't forget the **Rounded Bottom and Rounded Top patterns**, sometimes referred to as saucers or bowls. These patterns signal a gradual reversal of the prevailing trend, where a Rounded Top indicates a bearish reversal, and a Rounded Bottom signifies a bullish one. In a Rounded Top, the price action shows a slow, arching movement, indicating that bullish momentum is waning before reversing to a downtrend. The Rounded Bottom pattern mirrors this but in an inverted form, signaling a slow transition from bearish to bullish sentiment and is characterized by increasing volume as the price moves up.

Patterns like **Wedges** extend a bit more complexity but reward traders with substantial signals if identified correctly. Wedges come in two varieties: rising and falling. The *Rising Wedge* is often viewed as a bearish signal occurring within an uptrend, with converging trendlines sloping upwards. The *Falling Wedge* appears in a downtrend with converging trendlines sloping downwards, typically signaling a bullish reversal. These patterns indicate a slowing momentum, where price compression is expected to end with a breakout in the trend's opposite direction.

Understanding and spotting these patterns is foundational, but acting on them involves additional due diligence. While classical chart patterns provide structural insights into market sentiment and potential movements, integrating them with other analysis tools—like volume analysis and specific technical indicators—can improve their reliability. For example, a breakout from a head and shoulders pattern accompanied by increased volume adds credibility to the reversal signal.

As you become more adept at recognizing these patterns, it's crucial to maintain a disciplined approach. Patterns won't always play out as expected. Incorporating stop losses and being prepared for false breakouts can help manage risk. It's also beneficial to backtest patterns using historical data specific to the currency pairs you trade. This practice enables you to gauge the patterns' effectiveness within your trading system and adjust your strategies accordingly.

Lastly, remember that mastering classical chart patterns is not just about memorization but understanding the psychology and market dynamics they represent. Each pattern encapsulates collective trader behavior — fear, greed, anticipation — providing not only a forecast but a story of market sentiment. As you refine your ability to read these stories, blending structural analysis with real-time decision-making becomes second nature, ultimately contributing to a more nuanced and strategic trading approach.

Trend Analysis

In the realm of technical analysis mastery, understanding trends is paramount for effectively navigating the Forex market. Trend analysis allows traders to discern the overarching direction of the market, which can be bullish, bearish, or ranging. By identifying and following trends, traders can align their strategies to capitalize on prevailing market movements. This section delves into the tools and techniques vital for recognizing and confirming trends, such as trendlines and channels. Assessing the strength and sustainability of a trend can make the difference between a successful trade and a costly mistake. Through comprehensive trend analysis, traders enhance their ability to make informed decisions, anticipate potential reversals, and ultimately, increase their trading profitability.

Moving Averages are among the most versatile and widely-used tools in trend analysis, particularly in technical analysis for Forex traders. Understanding how to effectively apply moving averages can greatly enhance your ability to discern trends, identify potential entry and exit points, and increase overall trading profitability. Moving averages help smooth out price data, creating a single flowing line that can reveal the direction of the current trend while reducing the impact of random price fluctuations.

One of the most straightforward forms of moving averages is the Simple Moving Average (SMA). It's calculated by adding up the closing prices of a currency pair over a specific period and then dividing by the number of periods. For instance, a 20-day SMA averages the closing prices over the last 20 days. The simplicity of the SMA makes it a popular choice, but its main drawback is that it gives equal weight to all periods, potentially lagging behind timely market moves.

For those seeking more responsive measures, the Exponential Moving Average (EMA) might be more suitable. The EMA assigns more weight to recent price data, making it more sensitive to new information. This attribute allows traders to capture new trends faster and make more timely decisions, although it may also lead to more false signals during volatile market conditions. Balancing sensitivity and reliability becomes crucial in effectively utilizing moving averages.

Deciding between SMAs and EMAs often depends on your trading style and strategy. Short-term traders might favor EMAs to catch quick changes, while long-term traders may lean toward SMAs for a broader overview. Both types of moving averages can be implemented in conjunction, forming a robust system for trend analysis and signal confirmation.

Trading with moving averages becomes particularly powerful when combining multiple periods through techniques like the Dual Moving Average Crossover. In this context, you typically use a shorter-period moving average (e.g., 20-day) alongside a longer-period moving average (e.g., 50-day). When the shorter-term SMA crosses above the longer-term SMA, it generates a "Golden Cross" – a potential buy signal. Conversely, when it crosses below, it yields a "Death Cross," indicating a potential sell signal. These crossovers can provide clear, actionable insights, but they also require careful consideration of market context and additional confirmation indicators.

Another effective method involves the Moving Average Convergence Divergence (MACD) indicator, which leverages the principles of moving averages to gauge momentum. The MACD employs two EMAs and a signal line, interpreting the relationship between them to identify bullish or bearish movements. While detailed analysis of MACD falls under advanced indicators, understanding its foundation rooted in moving averages can enhance your approach to trend analysis.

Apart from crossovers, moving averages can also serve as dynamic support and resistance levels. Prices often “respect” these averages, especially during strong trends. For example, in an uptrend, the price might retrace to the SMA or EMA before resuming its upward movement, acting as a support. Conversely, in a downtrend, the moving average may act as a resistance barrier. Recognizing these interactions can help in making better-timed entries and exits.

Incorporating moving averages into your trading plan isn't without challenges. Market noise, sudden news events, and varying time frames can all impact the accuracy of signals generated by moving averages. Moreover, no single indicator should be used in isolation. Combining moving averages with other technical indicators, such as RSI or Bollinger Bands, can provide a more comprehensive view and enhance decision-making under different market conditions.

When diversifying your strategic arsenal, it's essential to perform backtesting using historical data to determine the effectiveness of moving averages in your specific trading environment. This process helps in fine-tuning parameters like periods and signal criteria, ensuring that you don't rely on an overly generalized approach. Furthermore, different currency pairs can exhibit varying behaviors that may necessitate tailored settings for moving averages.

Customization is key. Depending on volatility, trend strength, and your risk tolerance, you might prefer certain configurations over others. For instance, a trader focusing on high-volatility pairs like GBP/JPY might opt for shorter-period EMAs to capture swift movements, while a trader dealing with more stable pairs like EUR/USD may find longer-period SMAs more effective for identifying trends.

In real-world trading, emotional discipline plays a crucial role in utilizing moving averages effectively. Patience and consistency are paramount; sticking to your predefined rules and not second-guessing signals based on market noise can prevent irrational decisions. Equally important is keeping abreast of economic indicators and news events which might impact market trends, as these can offset the reliability of technical signals.

Finally, the flexibility offered by moving averages makes them suitable for various types of traders, from scalpers to swing and position traders. Their adaptability and ease of integration with other tools ensure that they remain a cornerstone of technical analysis. By mastering moving averages, you unlock a deeper understanding of market trends, ultimately helping to refine your strategies and enhance trading performance.

In summary, **Moving Averages** are indispensable tools in your technical analysis toolkit. Their ability to smooth price data, generate crossovers, and act as dynamic support and resistance levels offers myriad opportunities for identifying and confirming trends. As you integrate these insights into your broader trading strategy, remember that consistent practice, customization, and emotional discipline stand as pillars for successful implementation.

Support and Resistance Levels play a crucial role in *Trend Analysis*, offering intermediate to advanced Forex traders essential tools to identify key turning points in the market. A solid understanding of these concepts can significantly enhance a trader's ability to predict market behavior and make informed trading decisions. Support and resistance levels act as psychological barriers for traders, helping them identify where to enter and exit trades.

In essence, *support* refers to a price level where a downtrend can be expected to pause due to a concentration of demand. As the price decreases towards the support level, buyers become more likely to purchase the asset, mitigating further decline. Conversely, *resistance* is a price level where an uptrend can be expected to pause due to a concentration of supply. Here, sellers become more inclined to sell, preventing the price from rising further. Recognizing these levels enables traders to anticipate potential price movements, positioning themselves strategically in the market.

One effective method to identify support and resistance levels is by examining historical price charts. Historical highs and lows, as well as significant turning points, often serve as reliable indicators for future support and resistance levels. These historical levels highlight areas where traders have previously made strong buy or sell decisions, suggesting similar responses in the future. For instance, if a particular price level has repeatedly acted as a support or resistance in the past, it is likely to serve a similar role when revisited.

Moving averages also play a significant role in identifying support and resistance levels. By smoothing out price data, moving averages help traders observe the overarching trends and potential reversal points in the market. Shorter-term moving averages might signal dynamic support or resistance, adapting quickly to recent price changes. In contrast, longer-term moving averages provide more stable levels, often aligned with significant historical prices. Traders often look for confluences where moving averages intersect with historical support or resistance levels, marking these zones as high-probability areas for potential price reversals.

The concepts of *trendlines* and *channels* further augment the analysis of support and resistance levels. Trendlines are drawn by connecting successive highs or lows, providing a visual guideline for the direction of the trend. When a trendline aligns consistently with price movements, it forms a diagonal support or resistance level. Channels, formed by drawing parallel lines to a prevailing trendline, encompass the range within which prices fluctuate. Here, the upper line acts as resistance, while the lower line serves as support. Trading within these channels allows traders to capitalize on the price's oscillating movement while remaining aligned with the overall trend.

Another powerful tool for pinpointing support and resistance levels is the *Fibonacci retracement*. Based on the mathematical principles of the Fibonacci sequence, this tool helps in predicting potential reversal points by breaking down significant price movements into key levels, such as 23.6%, 38.2%, 50%, 61.8%, and 78.6%. These ratios are often observed in the financial markets, making them highly regarded among traders. By applying Fibonacci retracement lines to a chart, traders can identify areas where the price might find support or encounter resistance, thus offering strategic entry and exit points.

Volume, often overlooked, is a critical aspect when analyzing support and resistance levels. High trading volumes at specific levels indicate strong interest and conviction among traders, reinforcing the significance of those levels. For instance, if the price rebounds from a support level with a substantial increase in volume, it confirms the level's robustness and increases the likelihood of a continued uptrend. Conversely, a price rally turning down from a resistance level accompanied by heavy volume signals strong selling pressure, often preceding a downtrend.

Price action around support and resistance levels offers additional insights into market sentiment and potential price movements. Various candlestick patterns, such as hammers, dojis, and engulfing patterns, serve as valuable indicators of how the price might behave around these levels. For example, the formation of a hammer candlestick at a support level suggests strong buying interest, increasing the chances of a price rebound. Similarly, a bearish engulfing pattern at a resistance level signals potential downward pressure, alerting traders to a possible reversal.

Psychological factors cannot be ignored when discussing support and resistance levels. Round numbers, such as 1.0000 or 1.5000 in the Forex market, often emerge as significant psychological support and resistance levels. Traders tend to place orders around these figures, making them crucial focal points in market analysis. Awareness of these psychological levels helps traders anticipate market behavior and better align their strategies with the collective trading mindset.

Once support and resistance levels are identified, traders can use a variety of strategies to enhance their trading outcomes. One common approach is the *bounce strategy*, where traders enter positions when the price bounces off a support or resistance level. This strategy capitalizes on the anticipation of a price rebound, allowing traders to set tight stop-loss orders and maximize potential gains. The second approach is the *breakout strategy*, where traders seize opportunities when the price breaks through established support or resistance levels. Such breakouts often lead to significant price movements, driven by heightened market activity and strong momentum.

Combining support and resistance analysis with other technical indicators enhances the robustness of trading decisions. Indicators like the Relative Strength Index (RSI), Moving Average Convergence Divergence (MACD), and Bollinger Bands provide additional layers of confirmation for potential trade entries and exits. For instance, an RSI indicating overbought conditions near a resistance level strengthens the case for a potential sell trade. Similarly, a MACD crossover accompanied by a price break through a support level offers a potential signal for a short position.

Ultimately, mastering support and resistance levels in the context of trend analysis requires a blend of analytical skills, market awareness, and strategic thinking. By honing these abilities, traders can better navigate the Forex market, making well-informed decisions that harness the power of technical analysis. Over time, the proficiency in identifying and reacting to support and resistance levels can significantly contribute to a trader's overall profitability and success in the dynamic world of Forex trading.

Chapter 4: Advanced Use of Indicators

In this chapter, we'll delve deeper into the sophisticated utilization of indicators to enhance trading strategies for the keen Forex trader. Recognizing the vital distinction between leading and lagging indicators sets the stage for a more nuanced market analysis. Momentum and volume indicators like the MACD (Moving Average Convergence Divergence) will be examined to gauge the strength of market movements. We'll also explore the power of combining various indicators to generate more robust and reliable trading signals. This holistic approach not only sharpens your analytical skills but also aims to significantly bolster your trading performance through well-informed decision-making.

Leading vs. Lagging Indicators

Understanding the distinction between leading and lagging indicators is crucial for any trader looking to gain a deeper insight into the forex market. Essentially, these indicators help you determine market conditions and potential future movements. Recognizing when to use each type of indicator can significantly refine your trading strategy and increase your profitability.

Leading indicators are designed to anticipate potential trends and price movements ahead of time. They offer valuable signals that can give traders an edge by allowing them to enter or exit a trade before significant price movements occur. Some of the most commonly used leading indicators include the Relative Strength Index (RSI), Stochastic Oscillator, and various volume-based indicators.

Leading indicators, however, are not without their challenges. Because they aim to predict future movements, they can generate false signals. This means that relying solely on leading indicators can be risky; it necessitates a keen understanding of the market and the specific conditions under which these indicators tend to perform well.

On the other hand, **lagging indicators** follow market trends and provide signals after the trend or price movement has occurred. These indicators are particularly useful for confirming trends and ensuring that trading decisions are made based on established and verified movements. Common lagging indicators include Moving Averages (MA), Moving Average Convergence Divergence (MACD), and Bollinger Bands.

While lagging indicators are less prone to false signals compared to leading indicators, they do have the drawback of often being late to the party. This delay can result in missed opportunities, particularly in fast-moving markets where quick decision-making is crucial. However, they bring value in reducing the likelihood of whipsaw effects and confirming trends, thereby reducing the risk of acting on premature or false signals.

So, how does a trader decide between leading and lagging indicators? The answer lies in understanding the unique characteristics and current state of the market. For instance, in a ranging market where price movements are relatively contained within certain levels of support and resistance, leading indicators like the RSI or Stochastic Oscillator can be particularly effective. They can help identify overbought or oversold conditions, hinting at potential reversals before they occur.

In contrast, during a trending market where a clear direction is established, lagging indicators such as Moving Averages can be more useful. They help traders follow the trend with greater confidence, reducing the chances of premature exits. In these scenarios, lagging indicators can help traders stay with the trend until it shows signs of reversing.

But who says you have to choose solely between leading and lagging indicators? Many advanced traders effectively **combine both types** to create a more robust trading strategy. For example, one might use a leading indicator to generate a trade signal and then confirm that signal using a lagging indicator. This approach can help filter out false signals and provide a more reliable basis for trading decisions.

Think of the interplay between leading and lagging indicators like a dynamic duo in your trading toolkit. Leading indicators bring a proactive approach to spotting opportunities, while lagging indicators offer a more reactive but reliable method of confirming these opportunities. Together, they can create a balanced strategy that leverages the strengths of each type.

A practical application could look something like this: A trader notices a potential reversal in a currency pair based on the RSI indicating that the pair is in oversold territory (leading indicator). Before making a trading decision, the trader might wait for a short-term Moving Average to cross above a long-term Moving Average, thereby confirming the uptrend (lagging indicator).

It's also worth noting that adjusting the parameters of these indicators can further fine-tune their effectiveness. For instance, adjusting the length of Moving Averages or the periods used in the RSI calculation can tailor these indicators to different trading styles and market conditions.

The key takeaway here is that there's no one-size-fits-all approach to using leading and lagging indicators. The effectiveness of these tools depends largely on how well you understand their strengths, weaknesses, and appropriate applications within the context of your trading strategy. Advanced traders recognize the importance of continuous learning and adaptation, always seeking to refine their use of indicators based on evolving market conditions.

In conclusion, mastering the use of leading and lagging indicators is an ongoing process, requiring both theoretical understanding and practical application. By judiciously leveraging both types of indicators, traders can develop a more nuanced and effective trading strategy, thereby enhancing their ability to capture profitable opportunities while minimizing risks. Remember, the ultimate goal is to increase your trading precision and confidence, allowing you to navigate the ever-changing forex landscape with greater acumen.

Volume and Momentum Indicators

In the realm of advanced Forex trading, volume and momentum indicators offer invaluable insights into market dynamics, providing traders with the tools to gauge the strength and sustainability of price movements. Volume indicators help ascertain the level of activity behind price fluctuations, allowing you to discern whether a move is backed by robust trading interest or merely a fleeting spike. On the other hand, momentum indicators highlight the speed and intensity of price changes, offering clues about potential continuations or reversals in trend. When mastered, these indicators can be powerful allies in confirming patterns and trends identified through other analytical means, thereby enhancing the precision of your trading decisions. Knowing how to effectively integrate volume and momentum indicators into your strategy can give you a significant edge in the fast-paced world of Forex trading.

MACD (Moving Average Convergence Divergence) is a cornerstone of modern technical analysis, particularly in evaluating volume and momentum indicators. As an intermediate to advanced Forex trader, you probably know the importance of interpreting these indicators to refine your strategy and enhance your trade executions. With its ability to signal trend changes, overbought and oversold conditions, and even convergence and divergence of moving averages, MACD is a versatile tool worth mastering.

The MACD indicator consists of three main components: the MACD line, the signal line, and the histogram. The MACD line is derived by subtracting the 26-period Exponential Moving Average (EMA) from the 12-period EMA. The signal line, typically a 9-period EMA of the MACD line, serves as a trigger for buy and sell signals. The histogram, which represents the difference between the MACD line and the signal line, visually depicts the convergence or divergence between these two lines.

One of the primary advantages of using MACD is its ability to provide clear signals in both trending and ranging markets. When the MACD line crosses above the signal line, it generates a bullish signal indicating that it may be a good time to buy. Conversely, when the MACD line crosses below the signal line, it indicates a bearish signal, suggesting a selling opportunity. These crossovers can be even more significant when they occur above or below the zero line, which acts as an additional confirmation of the trend direction.

The zero line itself can serve as a critical pivot point for traders. When the MACD line is above the zero line, it suggests positive momentum, while a MACD line below the zero line implies negative momentum. By observing these conditions in conjunction with the price action, traders can make more informed decisions. For instance, a bullish crossover above the zero line signals strong upward momentum and can be a more reliable buying signal than a crossover below the zero line.

Volume and momentum are critical in Forex trading, and the MACD helps you discern the strength behind price movements. The histogram's bars visually represent the strength of the momentum, providing traders with another layer of analysis. Longer bars indicate stronger momentum, while shorter bars suggest weakening momentum. By paying attention to the histogram, traders can anticipate potential price reversals or continuations of the current trend.

Another key aspect of the MACD is its application in identifying divergences. Divergences occur when the price of a currency pair moves in the opposite direction of the MACD. This can signal a potential reversal of the current trend. For example, if the price is making higher highs while the MACD is making lower highs, this bearish divergence could indicate that the current uptrend is losing strength and a reversal may be imminent. Similarly, a bullish divergence occurs when the price makes lower lows but the MACD makes higher lows.

Using MACD effectively requires an understanding of its strengths and limitations. It's crucial to avoid relying solely on MACD signals without considering other factors like overall market conditions and other technical indicators. While the MACD is potent, integrating it with other indicators, such as the Relative Strength Index (RSI) or volume indicators like On-Balance Volume (OBV), can provide a more comprehensive view.

For a more advanced usage, some traders employ the MACD histogram to devise dynamic trading strategies. Instead of merely focusing on crossovers, they look for histogram bars that show signs of momentum acceleration or deceleration. This nuanced approach can help in identifying subtle shifts in market sentiment, enabling you to stay ahead of the curve.

Trading is inherently about managing probabilities, and the MACD is no silver bullet. False signals can and do occur, especially in choppy or sideways markets. It's essential to have a solid risk management strategy in place. Incorporate stop-loss orders, and never over-leverage your positions based on a single indicator. Keep in mind the broader picture and align your MACD analysis with other indicators and fundamental analysis for the most reliable outcomes.

Customization of the MACD settings can also lead to more tailored signals based on your specific trading style. While the default settings (12, 26, 9) are widely used, some traders find success by adjusting these periods to better align with their trading horizon and the volatility of the specific currency pair they are trading.

Lastly, continually backtest your strategies using historical data to see how they would have performed in different market conditions. The MACD's effectiveness can vary with timeframes and market environments, so thorough backtesting can provide valuable insights and help in fine-tuning your approach.

In summary, incorporating MACD into your trade analysis can significantly enhance your ability to identify profitable trading opportunities by gauging market momentum and volume. By understanding its components and how to interpret its signals effectively, you'll be better equipped to make informed trading decisions. Remember, while MACD is a powerful tool, its true potential is realized when used in conjunction with other analytical methods and a robust risk management plan.

Combining Indicators for Enhanced Signals

Combining indicators for enhanced trading signals is an essential skill for intermediate to advanced Forex traders. Relying on just one indicator can lead to missed opportunities or false signals, which is why integrating multiple indicators can significantly improve the accuracy and reliability of your trading decisions. By doing this effectively, you can create a more robust trading strategy that can adapt to different market conditions, helping to increase profitability and manage risks better.

First, it's important to understand the types of indicators you're working with. Indicators generally fall into two main categories: leading and lagging. Leading indicators aim to predict future price movements and are often used in conjunction with lagging indicators, which confirm trends and validate signals. For example, the Relative Strength Index (RSI) is a leading indicator that can signal overbought or oversold conditions, while the Moving Average Convergence Divergence (MACD) is a lagging indicator that helps to confirm the trend's direction and strength. Utilizing these indicators together can provide a more comprehensive view of the market.

One effective method is to combine an oscillator (leading indicator) with a trend-following indicator (lagging indicator). This duo can help you identify both the trend direction and the timing of market entries and exits. Take RSI and MACD, for instance. The RSI can help you determine whether a currency pair is overbought or oversold, signaling a potential reversal. The MACD can then confirm this signal by showing that a trend change is indeed occurring.

When using multiple indicators, it's crucial to avoid overloading your charts with too many lines and gauges. This can lead to analysis paralysis, where you become overwhelmed by conflicting information. Keep your chart clean and only use the indicators that are most relevant to your trading strategy. For example, combining just the MACD and RSI can provide sufficient insights without cluttering your workspace.

Another powerful combination is the integration of volume indicators with momentum indicators. Volume indicators, such as the On-Balance Volume (OBV), provide insights into the strength of a price move, while momentum indicators, like the Stochastic Oscillator, gauge the speed and change of price movements. When these indicators are aligned, and both indicate either buying or selling pressure, the signal's reliability increases.

A practical application of combining indicators can be seen in trend continuation trades. Suppose you've identified a strong uptrend using a moving average cross-over (a lagging indicator). By applying the RSI (a leading indicator), you can wait for the RSI to dip below a certain level (e.g., 30) before initiating a buy order, expecting the trend to continue upwards. This method helps you capitalize on brief counter-trend moves within a broader trend, maximizing profit potential.

Additionally, integrating support and resistance levels with your chosen indicators can further enhance your signal accuracy. Support and resistance levels represent psychological price points where buying or selling pressure is typically high. Combining these levels with indicators like Bollinger Bands can help determine potential breakout or reversal points. For instance, if the price touches a lower Bollinger Band at a well-established support level, this confluence can signify a high-probability buying opportunity.

To better understand how these combinations work in practice, consider the following example of a multi-indicator strategy:

- **Step 1:** Identify the overarching trend using a long-term moving average, such as the 200-day SMA. This sets the context for your trades.

- **Step 2:** Use the MACD to confirm the trend direction. If the MACD line crosses above the signal line while above zero, it reinforces a bullish trend.
- **Step 3:** Apply the RSI to find entry points. Wait for the RSI to drop below 30 and then rise above it, indicating oversold conditions in an uptrend.
- **Step 4:** Check OBV to see if it confirms the potential move. If the OBV is rising, it suggests that volume supports the price increase, validating your entry signal.

This structured approach demonstrates how combining multiple indicators can give a more comprehensive and nuanced view, increasing your chances of making successful trades.

While combining indicators, always remain aware of potential pitfalls. One of the biggest challenges is avoiding confirmation bias. Traders might selectively interpret signals to confirm their preconceived notions, leading to erroneous trades. To mitigate this, strictly adhere to predefined criteria for your indicator combinations and avoid making impulsive decisions based on partial signals.

Backtesting your multi-indicator strategy is a non-negotiable step in ensuring its effectiveness. Use historical data to test how well your indicator combinations would have performed in various market conditions. This process gives you insight into the strategy's strengths and weaknesses, enabling you to fine-tune it before using it in live trading.

Remember, no combination of indicators is infallible. Market dynamics are complex and ever-changing, necessitating continuous learning and adaptation. Consider expanding your toolkit by exploring other technical indicators and adjusting your combinations based on evolving market patterns. Techniques like machine learning can also be employed to find optimal indicator combinations, but that's a topic for more advanced traders.

In conclusion, effectively combining indicators for enhanced signals involves a blend of understanding each tool's unique strengths and adopting a disciplined, systematic approach. By doing so, traders can improve signal accuracy, better manage risk, and ultimately boost their trading performance.

Chapter 5: The Power of Price Action

Transition from reliance on indicators and immerse yourself in the raw, unfiltered movements of the market through the study of price action. This approach allows traders to interpret the market's intention by observing price movements over time, without the lag commonly associated with indicators. Price action strategies like the Pin Bar and Inside Bar signal pivotal market turning points by highlighting key support and resistance zones. Engulfing patterns and false breaks offer crucial insights into market momentum and potential reversals. Mastering these techniques enhances a trader's ability to read market sentiment directly from price charts, promoting a more intuitive and responsive trading style.

Reading the Market Without Indicators

Forex trading can often feel like an unwieldy beast, especially when you're bombarded with the myriad of indicators out there purporting to predict market movements. But if you peel back the layers of complexity, you'll find that price action itself offers a wealth of information. This approach doesn't just strip away the noise; it brings you closer to the raw dynamics of the market.

Understanding price action is akin to learning a new language. The market speaks through its price movements. Learning to read these movements can give you a clearer picture, often more reliable than when you're bogged down with too many indicators. At its core, price action is straightforward but requires a keen eye and understanding to interpret effectively.

When you analyze the market without indicators, you're focusing on actual price movements as they relate to historical prices. The simplest elements include the open, high, low, and close prices of a trading period. Paying attention to these can help you discern the strength or weakness of a price move, prevailing trends, and potential reversals. Remember, every candlestick on your chart is a story of what the market is doing.

For instance, a long wick on a candlestick might signify strong rejection of a certain price level. The market tested that price but quickly moved back, indicating that traders weren't willing to deal at that price point. Such observations can be crucial in predicting future price behavior.

Traders who excel in reading price action often spot patterns that reveal the market's intentions. Double tops and bottoms, head and shoulders formations, and other such patterns are more than just visual shapes—they are deep-seated expressions of market psychology. Recognizing these patterns allows you to anticipate future movements with a level of precision that can sometimes surpass those using complex indicators.

Another powerful aspect of price action is the ability to identify support and resistance levels. These are essentially price points where the market repeatedly struggles to move past, either upward (resistance) or downward (support). By keeping an eye on these levels, you can gauge where the price might reverse or continue its trend. This not only helps in setting entry and exit points but also assists in managing risk effectively.

Begin by focusing on key levels. Look at historical highs and lows, significant round numbers, and areas where price has changed direction multiple times. These zones often act as psychological barriers for traders and are crucial in determining market sentiment.

It's also beneficial to observe the speed and momentum of price movements. Rapid price changes can indicate strong buying or selling interest and typically precede significant trend changes. Conversely, when price creeps slowly, it often suggests market indecision, potentially signaling a pending consolidation or reversal.

One essential aspect to master in price action trading is the concept of market structure. Market structure refers to the recurring patterns and behaviors that prices exhibit over time. Analyzing higher highs and higher lows in an uptrend, or lower highs and lower lows in a downtrend, gives you a clear framework to understand trend progression and potential reversal signals.

Take, for example, an uptrend characterized by periodic pullbacks. When the price doesn't pull back as deep as it did previously, it can be a sign that the trend is gaining strength. Conversely, a deeper pullback than usual may indicate looming weakness. These nuances in market structure are gold mines for the discerning trader.

Additionally, price action allows you to read the market's mood by watching for certain candlestick patterns. A pin bar, showing a significant price rejection, or an engulfing candlestick, indicating strong momentum, can speak volumes. These patterns, when viewed in context with the broader market structure, can give you incredibly accurate signals for entry or exit.

Keep in mind that the reliability of these patterns often increases when they form at significant support or resistance levels or align with the prevailing trend. It's about context. A bullish engulfing pattern at a strong support level carries more weight than the same pattern in the middle of a choppy range.

One of the powerful advantages of reading price action without indicators is that it places you in sync with the market's rhythm. You learn to respond to what is actually happening rather than what might happen. This approach reduces lag and improves your reaction time—crucial for short-term trading where every pip counts.

It's important to stress, however, that price action trading isn't about forsaking all tools in your trading toolbox. Think of it as another technique that complements your existing strategies. It can work in tandem with other forms of analysis, like understanding the broader economic landscape or utilizing indicators sparingly to confirm what price action is already telling you.

Many traders make the mistake of applying price action methods in isolation without grasping the larger market context. For instance, trading off a pin bar in a low-volume market might not yield the same results as in a high-volume market. Volume, sentiment, and fundamental news should also be factored into your analysis.

In a nutshell, mastering the art of reading the market without indicators calls for practice, patience, and persistent learning. It's less about being right all the time and more about developing an intuitive grasp of market movements. By sharpening this skill, you'll not only enhance your trading accuracy but also bolster your confidence, setting the stage for sustained profitability.

Take your time to study charts, recognize patterns, and observe how price reacts at different levels. Over time, these observations will become second nature, allowing you to make trading decisions with increased speed and efficiency. In the end, price action, in its simplicity and elegance, remains one of the most powerful tools in a trader's arsenal.

Pin Bar and Inside Bar Strategies

When it comes to price action trading, Pin Bar and Inside Bar strategies hold a significant place. These patterns give traders the confidence to make calculated decisions based on the raw movements of price, rather than relying solely on indicators. They enable traders to decipher market sentiment and predict future price action more accurately.

First, let's delve into Pin Bars. Also known as Pinocchio Bars, Pin Bars are named for their long wicks and tiny bodies. The wick, resembling a nose that's sticking out, represents a price rejection that might indicate a strong reversal signal. What makes Pin Bars compelling is their ability to demonstrate clear rejections of price levels, offering a robust cue for entering trades.

For a Pin Bar to be valid, it generally needs to have a long wick making up at least two-thirds of the entire bar's length. The body should be small and the open and close of the bar should be close to one end of the range. This structure conveys the story: the market attempted to push prices in one direction but faced strong opposition, returning to nearly the same level it started. Consequently, a bearish Pin Bar indicates rejection of higher prices and a potential downward move, while a bullish Pin Bar signifies rejection of lower prices and potential upward movement.

Recognizing Pin Bars is only the first step. The strategic application of these patterns involves understanding where they appear on the chart. Pin Bars occurring at key support and resistance levels, trend lines, or after extended trends, are far more reliable signals than those appearing in the middle of congestion areas. For instance, a bullish Pin Bar showing at a fundamental support level after a downtrend provides a powerful signal of an impending upward movement.

Combining Pin Bar recognition with other price action patterns or technical indicators significantly enhances trading accuracy. For example, aligning a Pin Bar setup with moving averages or alongside a confluence of Fibonacci levels can validate the trade setup. This confluence principle taps into the collective agreement of different analytical tools to form a high-probability trade.

Now, let's transition to Inside Bars, another powerful price action pattern. An Inside Bar signifies market consolidation, often acting as a precursor to a breakout. It's a candlestick pattern where the current bar is entirely contained within the high and low range of the preceding bar. Metaphorically speaking, it's a pause for breath in market movement.

Inside Bars typically show up after a strong trend, indicating that the market is taking a breather before continuing in the same direction or possibly reversing. The beauty of Inside Bars is that they can serve as both continuation and reversal signals, but interpreting them correctly requires context. A trend-following trade out of an Inside Bar is often the safer bet, as it harmonizes with the prevailing market momentum.

To trade Inside Bars effectively, it's crucial to watch for breakouts from these bars. A breakout could occur in either direction, signaling potential trading opportunities. Placing entry orders just beyond the high and low of the Inside Bar allows traders to capitalize on the impending volatility burst. Moreover, stop-loss orders could be strategically set at the opposite side of the Inside Bar, thus minimizing potential losses.

A valuable tip for trading Inside Bars is waiting for a false breakout or a second bar within the Inside Bar before making entry decisions. This conservative approach increases the likelihood of filtering out false signals. Essentially, if the price breaks in one direction and swiftly reverses, it's typically an indication that the real breakout could be imminent in the opposite direction.

The incorporation of Pin Bar and Inside Bar strategies into one's trading toolbox lays the groundwork for understanding market dynamics on a deeper level. These strategies represent market psychology in its purest form, capturing the battle between buyers and sellers. While Pin Bars convey abrupt rejections and potential reversals, Inside Bars illustrate consolidation and pending breakouts.

Incorporating these strategies demands practice and experience, just like any other trading methodology. Traders can refine their skills by back-testing these patterns on historical data and placing them in a simulated trading environment before going live. It's also crucial to integrate sound risk management practices, ensuring that each trade is part of a larger, well-thought-out plan.

Moreover, both Pin Bar and Inside Bar strategies can be combined with other forms of analysis for greater effectiveness. Using them alongside volume analysis, support and resistance levels, or even trend lines, can provide further confirmation and strengthen the case for a particular trade setup.

In conclusion, the brilliance of Pin Bar and Inside Bar strategies lies in their simplicity and their grounding in price action. They empower traders to make informed decisions by observing the very essence of market movements. For intermediate and advanced Forex traders aiming to refine their craft, mastering these patterns is not just beneficial but essential. Consistent practice, along with a disciplined approach to risk management, will pave the way for more profitable and confident trading.

Engulfing Patterns and False Breaks

Engulfing patterns and false breaks are among the most powerful price action signals a Forex trader can wield. Understanding these patterns not only enhances your ability to read the market but also helps in making more informed trading decisions. Let's start with engulfing patterns.

An engulfing pattern is a two-candle reversal pattern that can appear at the end of both uptrends and downtrends. Essentially, the body of the second candle fully engulfs the body of the first one. It's a clear signal of a potential reversal. There are two types: bullish engulfing and bearish engulfing. A bullish engulfing pattern occurs at the end of a downtrend and a bearish engulfing at the end of an uptrend.

To identify a bullish engulfing pattern, look for a smaller bearish candle (first candle) followed by a larger bullish candle (second candle) that completely envelops the first candle's body. This pattern indicates a shift in momentum from sellers to buyers, suggesting that the market may be heading upward.

Similarly, a bearish engulfing pattern happens when a smaller bullish candle is followed by a larger bearish candle, signaling that sellers might be taking control. It's a strong indication that the market may turn downward. Recognizing these patterns can help traders make better entries and exits.

However, like any other trading signals, engulfing patterns are most effective when combined with other forms of analysis. Context is critical here. An engulfing pattern observed at key support or resistance levels becomes more significant. Likewise, confirming signals from indicators like RSI or MACD can add another layer of reliability.

False breaks, on the other hand, can be both a bane and a boon to traders. A false break occurs when the price breaches a significant support or resistance level but fails to maintain momentum in that direction. Many traders are often caught off-guard by false breaks, which can lead to unnecessary stop-outs and losses.

Incorporating false breaks into your trading strategy involves a mix of patience and precision. It's essential to understand that false breaks often generate opportunities. They can indicate that the original trend is still valid, thus providing high-probability reentry points.

One approach to dealing with false breaks is to wait for a confirmation. Instead of entering immediately after the price breaks a level, wait for the candle to close beyond that level. This additional step can filter out a lot of false signals and save you from many losing trades.

Another effective tactic is to use stop-loss orders more strategically. Placing your stop-loss just beyond the level of a false break can provide that extra bit of protection, ensuring you're not taken out of a trade prematurely. Think of it as a way to give your trades some breathing room.

Engulfing patterns and false breaks can also be especially effective when used together. Imagine you spot a false break below a support level followed by a bullish engulfing pattern. This setup can provide a powerful signal that the market is likely to reverse upward, giving you an excellent entry point.

Here's a practical example: Suppose EUR/USD is trending downward and approaches a significant support level around 1.1000. The price briefly dips below 1.1000 but quickly rebounds, forming a false break. The next candle is a bullish engulfing pattern. This combination suggests that the downward momentum has faded, and the bulls are gaining control. A savvy trader would recognize this as an opportunity to go long with a tight stop-loss just below the false break's low.

It's also worth noting that false breaks aren't just limited to horizontal support and resistance levels. They can occur with trend lines, moving averages, and other dynamic support and resistance zones. Therefore, integrating these concepts into your overall price action strategy can significantly enhance your trading edge.

Some traders find visualizing these patterns on different time frames helpful. For instance, the reliability of an engulfing pattern or a false break might increase when observed on larger time frames like the 4-hour or daily chart. These higher time frames often filter out "market noise" and provide more reliable signals.

To sum it up, mastering engulfing patterns and false breaks involves a keen eye for detail, solid understanding of market structures, and strategic application of technical tools. They are not standalone strategies but work best when integrated into a comprehensive trading plan.

If you practice diligently and refine your approach, you'll likely find that these patterns can significantly boost your trading performance, helping you stay ahead of the curve in the ever-volatile Forex market.

The next section will delve into another powerful price action strategy: Pin Bar and Inside Bar Strategies. These too can complement the lessons learned on engulfing patterns and false breaks, creating a robust framework for improved trading outcomes.

Chapter 6: Risk Management Techniques

Effective risk management is the cornerstone of successful Forex trading, especially for seasoned traders aiming to optimize their profitability. At its core, risk management involves making calculated decisions to minimize potential losses while maximizing gains. Techniques such as understanding and managing leverage allow traders to control larger positions with a smaller amount of capital, though this also increases potential risk. Implementing stop loss and take profit strategies is crucial for protecting your investment and ensuring disciplined exits, whether the market moves in your favor or against you. Moreover, the importance of position sizing cannot be overstated—it's essential to determine the right amount of capital to allocate per trade to avoid risking too much on any single trade. These strategies, when combined, create a robust risk management framework that can enhance trading performance and significantly reduce emotional decision-making under pressure.

Understanding and Managing Leverage

Leverage is a double-edged sword in Forex trading. It can dramatically amplify your profits, but it can just as quickly magnify your losses if not managed correctly. Understanding leverage and effectively managing it are crucial skills for intermediate to advanced traders aiming for consistent profitability.

First, let's clarify what leverage is. In simple terms, leverage allows you to control a large position with a relatively small amount of capital. For example, if your broker offers 100:1 leverage, you can control $100,000 worth of currency with just $1,000. This can make the Forex market accessible to those with limited capital, but it also introduces a significant element of risk.

When using leverage, it's essential to strike a balance between potential gains and the risk of substantial losses. High leverage can lead to large profits, but it also means that even small market movements can result in significant losses. Hence, managing leverage involves understanding how much leverage to use in different market conditions and adjusting your strategies accordingly.

One of the first steps in managing your leverage is recognizing your risk tolerance. Are you comfortable with the possibility of losing a significant portion of your account in a short time, or do you prefer a more conservative approach? Your risk tolerance will dictate how much leverage you should use. Traders with a lower risk tolerance should consider using lower leverage, whereas those with a higher risk tolerance might be inclined to use more.

Perhaps the most important aspect of managing leverage is implementing stringent risk management measures. These include setting stop-loss orders to prevent runaway losses and using take-profit orders to secure gains. A well-placed stop-loss order ensures that you exit a position before it can cause significant damage to your account balance. Similarly, a take-profit order helps lock in profits before market conditions change unfavorably.

Position sizing is another key component of managing leverage. It involves determining the appropriate amount to trade relative to the size of your account. By using proper position sizing, you ensure that you do not overexpose your account to risk. It's a strategy that involves careful calculation and discipline, ensuring that each trade aligns with your overall risk management plan.

Leverage also requires a solid understanding of market conditions. Different market environments may necessitate different leverage levels. For instance, during periods of high volatility, a lower leverage might be more appropriate to prevent large swings from wiping out your account. Conversely, in a stable market, you might opt for higher leverage to maximize profits.

It's crucial to continually monitor and adjust your leverage as your account grows or as market conditions change. This adaptive approach helps mitigate risks associated with varying market situations. For instance, if you start with $10,000 and see substantial growth to $50,000, the leverage you initially used might need to be adjusted. Similarly, if you experience a drawdown, reducing your leverage can help protect your remaining capital.

Emotional discipline plays a vital role when dealing with leverage. High leverage can tempt traders into executing larger-than-usual trades, driven by the potential for significant gains. However, this can lead to emotional trading, where decisions are guided by greed or fear rather than sound analysis. Maintaining emotional control and sticking to your trading plan are essential for leveraging effectively and sustainably.

A recommendation for advanced traders is to incorporate regular reviews of your leverage strategy. Analyzing past trades and their outcomes can provide valuable insights into how effectively you've managed leverage. Look for patterns or common factors in your profitable and losing trades. This analysis can help you refine your approach and make more informed decisions moving forward.

Furthermore, consider the impact of leverage on your overall trading psychology. High leverage can create pressure, leading to stress and potentially clouding your judgment. It's essential to recognize this and take steps to maintain a clear, focused mindset. This might involve taking breaks, practicing mindfulness, or even seeking professional guidance to improve your trading psychology.

In summary, understanding and managing leverage in Forex trading requires a comprehensive approach. It involves recognizing your risk tolerance, implementing strict risk management, practicing proper position sizing, adjusting to market conditions, maintaining emotional discipline, and regular review. By mastering these aspects, you can harness the power of leverage to enhance your trading performance and profitability while minimizing the associated risks.

Stop Loss and Take Profit Strategies

When it comes to risk management, few tools are as vital to an intermediate or advanced Forex trader as stop loss and take profit strategies. These strategies not only help in protecting capital but also in optimizing gains by managing market volatility. Let's delve into the importance, implementation, and best practices of executing these crucial elements of risk management.

The core principle behind a *stop loss* order is simple: it minimizes losses by automatically exiting a trade when the market moves against you by a predefined amount. Picture this: you've conducted your analysis, executed a trade, but the market starts moving unfavorably. Rather than manually monitoring the trade and risking a significant drawdown, a stop loss order ensures that your loss is cut off at a level you're comfortable with.

On the other hand, a *take profit* order works to automatically close a position once a certain level of profit has been achieved. This helps in locking in profits without continuously monitoring the market. In a fast-paced trading environment, knowing when to take your gains off the table can often be the difference between a winning strategy and potential losses due to market reversals.

Properly setting stop loss and take profit levels requires more than just picking arbitrary numbers. Successful traders employ a blend of technical analysis, market sentiment, and risk-reward ratios to determine these levels. For instance, using support and resistance levels can be an excellent way to set stop losses. If a trade dips below a key support level, it could indicate a continued downward trend, thereby triggering your stop loss to prevent further losses.

Another effective approach is utilizing ATR (Average True Range) to measure market volatility. By setting your stop loss based on a multiple of the ATR, you can allow for normal market fluctuations without being prematurely stopped out. This method is particularly useful in volatile periods where wide price swings are not necessarily indicative of a trend reversal.

When it comes to take profit orders, aligning them with significant resistance levels or Fibonacci retracement levels can be highly effective. If you're bullish and notice a resistance level that the price has struggled to break in the past, it might serve as an ideal take profit point. Equally, for bearish trades, recognizing support levels where the price has previously bounced back can provide excellent take profit targets.

The risk-reward ratio is another cornerstone in setting stop loss and take profit levels. A common rule is to aim for a risk-reward ratio of at least 1:2. This ensures that the potential profit from a trade outweighs the potential loss, providing a buffer that can make a trading strategy successful over time. For example, if your stop loss is set at 20 pips, your take profit should ideally be set at 40 pips.

Sound execution of stop loss and take profit strategies also demands adaptability. Market conditions are ever-changing, and what worked yesterday might not be effective today. Trailing stop losses add this dynamic element by adjusting the stop loss level as the market moves in your favor. This ensures that you lock in profits as the trade becomes more favorable, all while providing a safety net against reversals.

Implementing multiple take profit levels can also be beneficial. This technique involves setting take profit orders at various price levels. For instance, if you're long on a currency pair, you might take partial profits at the first resistance level and set another take profit order at a higher resistance level. This allows you to capitalize on the initial move while also leaving room for further gains if the trend continues.

Moreover, combining these strategies with psychological discipline is crucial. The human element plays a significant role in trading; fear and greed can cloud judgment, leading to impulsive decisions. Sticking to predetermined stop loss and take profit levels helps mitigate emotional biases, reinforcing a disciplined approach to trading.

Yet, even with the best planning, unforeseen market events can occur, rendering your stop loss orders susceptible to slippage, particularly in volatile markets. It's essential for traders to use reputable brokers with efficient execution policies. Some advanced traders also employ guaranteed stop losses, which ensure that their positions are closed at the exact stop loss level, regardless of market gaps or slippage.

Furthermore, backtesting your stop loss and take profit strategies cannot be overstated. By testing these levels across historical data, you're better equipped to understand how they would perform under different market scenarios. This provides invaluable insights, allowing necessary tweaks to optimize performance before employing these strategies in live markets.

In conclusion, mastering stop loss and take profit strategies is indispensable for any intermediate or advanced Forex trader. They help manage risk, protect your capital, and lock in profits, all while allowing you to trade with greater confidence and less emotional stress.

When you combine these strategies with robust technical analysis, a disciplined mindset, and continuous adaptation, you're well on your way to achieving long-term success in Forex trading.

The Importance of Position Sizing

Position sizing isn't just another box to tick in your trading plan; it's a critical component of risk management that can make or break your trading career. Imagine you've identified a stellar trade setup: everything lines up, from technical indicators to market sentiment. But if your position size is too large, a single adverse move can wipe out a significant portion of your trading capital. Conversely, if your position size is too small, the potential profit won't justify your time and effort. Striking the right balance is key.

Let's get into the heart of why position sizing is non-negotiable for serious Forex traders. It allows you to manage your risk effectively by limiting the potential loss on any given trade. You see, the Forex market is notoriously volatile, and prices can swing dramatically within minutes. Before you even think about clicking the "buy" or "sell" button, you need to determine how much of your capital you're willing to risk on that trade.

One common guideline many traders follow is the 1-2% rule. This rule suggests that you should risk no more than 1-2% of your trading account on a single trade. For example, if you have a $10,000 account, you'd risk no more than $100 to $200 on any trade. This way, even a series of losing trades won't decimate your account, giving you the longevity to ride through bad streaks and capitalize on good ones.

Why does this matter so much in Forex trading? The market movements are unpredictable, and even the best setups can fail due to unforeseen circumstances. By limiting your risk, you're effectively ensuring that a single trade won't take you out of the game. Consistency is key, and position sizing helps you maintain it.

Let's delve deeper into some techniques for calculating position size. At the core, the size of your position should be determined by your risk per trade and your stop-loss distance. If you're risking 1%, figure out what 1% of your total capital is. Then, determine how far your stop loss will be from your entry point. The further away your stop loss, the smaller your position size should be to maintain your risk within the desired limit.

For instance, you want to risk 1% of a $10,000 account. That equates to $100 per trade. If your stop loss is set 50 pips away from your entry point, you need to calculate how many lots will make a 50-pip move equal to $100. In this scenario, if you're trading a pair where 1 pip equals $10 for a standard lot, you'd trade two mini lots (0.2 standard lots) to keep your risk within the $100 limit.

This method ensures you dynamically adjust your position size based on the specifics of each trade rather than a fixed amount each time. It's a more sophisticated approach that aligns with varying market conditions and trading strategies.

Aside from limiting risk, proper position sizing also helps you optimize returns. By adopting a methodical approach to position sizing, you can focus on high-probability setups without fear of losing big or missing out on lucrative opportunities. It's a strategy that bridges caution with the potential for healthy profits.

Many traders make the mistake of not adapting their position size to the unique aspects of each trade, resulting in inconsistent performance. The market is not static; it varies in volatility, trend strength, and underlying conditions. Therefore, your position sizes should also be flexible.

Let's not forget about leverage. Leverage allows you to control a larger position with a smaller amount of your own money. While this can magnify gains, it also magnifies losses. Proper position sizing takes into account the amount of leverage being used. High leverage can quickly turn a manageable losing trade into a catastrophic one if position size is not properly controlled. Always keep in mind that leverage is a double-edged sword.

Experienced traders often use a position size calculator or trading platforms that automatically calculate the appropriate lot size based on the predefined risk percentage and stop loss. This technology saves time and reduces the chance for manual error, making it easier to maintain discipline in size management.

Incorporating position sizing into your risk management strategy isn't a one-time task. It requires ongoing attention and adjustment as your account size changes and as you refine your overall trading strategy. Regularly revisiting and recalibrating your position sizes is essential to staying aligned with your risk tolerance and market conditions.

Ultimately, the importance of position sizing can't be overstated. It's not just about protecting your account balance; it's about cultivating a mindset of measured, calculated risks that lead to long-term profitability. By meticulously controlling how much you put on the line in each trade, you position yourself not just to survive in the Forex market, but to thrive.

Chapter 7: Trading Psychology and Mindset

Trading psychology and mindset are critical components that often separate successful traders from those consistently facing losses. It's all about understanding the emotional pitfalls and mental hurdles intrinsic to trading. Recognizing and overcoming emotional trading, like the fear of missing out (FOMO) or the impulse to revenge-trade after a loss, is paramount. Confidence in your strategy, combined with patience, allows you to endure the ups and downs of forex trading without making rash decisions. Developing a disciplined trader's mindset involves continuous self-reflection and mental conditioning, ensuring that each trade is executed based on logical analysis rather than emotional reactions. Remember, it's about making informed decisions and sticking to your plan, even when the market tempts you to act impulsively.

Overcoming Emotional Trading

Trading psychology is one of the cornerstones of successful Forex trading. As an intermediate or advanced trader, you're already familiar with the basics and more sophisticated trading strategies. However, no matter how advanced your techniques are, emotional trading can undermine your success. Emotional trading occurs when decisions are based on psychological factors rather than rational analysis. This section aims to explore ways to mitigate these emotional pitfalls and make more disciplined, calculated decisions.

Firstly, it's essential to recognize the presence of emotions in trading. Common emotions that impact traders include fear, greed, excitement, and frustration. These feelings don't just appear out of nowhere; they emerge from unpredictable market movements, previous trading experiences, and financial stakes. Awareness is the first step toward overcoming emotional trading. The ability to acknowledge when you're acting emotionally rather than logically can serve as a critical checkpoint before executing any trade.

One effective method to keep emotions in check is to develop and stick to a well-defined trading plan. Your trading plan should outline your strategy, risk parameters, entry and exit rules, and even your goals. When you have a robust plan, you're more likely to follow it rather than make impulsive decisions. This structured approach fosters discipline, which is essential for overcoming emotional trading.

Some traders find that journaling their trades helps them identify emotional patterns. Keeping a trade journal allows you to record every trade, including the reasoning behind it and its outcome. Over time, you'll be able to pinpoint when you're most susceptible to emotional trading. While this might seem time-consuming, the insights gained are invaluable. For example, if you find that you often make poor decisions after a losing streak, you can implement stricter guidelines to avoid trading during these times.

Mindset and mental conditioning play significant roles in managing emotions. Practices such as mindfulness and meditation can help traders stay calm and focused. Taking regular breaks can also prevent emotional fatigue, which can cloud your judgment. Remember, trading is as much a mental game as it is about market analysis.

Risk management is crucial in mitigating the impact of emotions on trading. Setting predefined stop-loss and take-profit levels can limit your exposure to large losses and take the emotional aspect out of deciding when to exit a position. Many professional traders recommend never risking more than 1-2% of your trading capital on a single trade. This approach not only protects your account but also makes it easier to handle losses emotionally, knowing that your risk is controlled.

Let's delve into fear and greed, two of the most potent emotions that affect traders. Fear can prevent you from entering potentially profitable trades or cause you to exit trades prematurely. On the other hand, greed can push you to hold on to positions longer than advisable, hoping for greater gains, or take unnecessary risks. Both emotions can be mitigated by adhering to your trading plan and using tools like stop-loss orders. If fear of losing is too overwhelming, it might be helpful to revisit your risk management strategy and ensure you're comfortable with the amounts at stake.

Another emotion that can wreak havoc on your trading is frustration. It mostly arises after a series of losses, leading traders to revenge trade in an attempt to recover lost funds. This emotion-driven trading can often result in more significant losses and further frustration. To combat this, you need to accept that losses are part of trading. No strategy has a 100% win rate. The sooner you accept this and move on from losses without letting them influence your future trades, the better off you'll be.

Some traders benefit from setting a cooling-off period after a loss. For instance, if you experience a significant loss, give yourself a set amount of time, say 24 hours, before you make another trade. This practice helps you cool down emotionally and approach the market with a fresh perspective.

Furthermore, realistic goal setting can help to manage emotional highs and lows. Unrealistic expectations can lead to severe emotional swings that can negatively impact your trading decisions. Set achievable, incremental goals, and celebrate small victories. This approach not only builds confidence but also makes it easier to stick to your trading plan.

Confidence and patience also play essential roles in trading psychology. Lack of confidence can lead to second-guessing and missed opportunities, while overconfidence can result in reckless trading. The key is to find a balanced approach by continuously refining your skills and learning from every trade, regardless of its outcome. Patience is crucial because not every day will present a trading opportunity that fits your strategy. Waiting for the right conditions is often more profitable than constant action.

Your environment can also affect your emotional state and trading performance. A cluttered or noisy workspace can contribute to stress and distraction. Creating a dedicated, organized trading space can make a substantial difference. Additionally, surrounding yourself with like-minded individuals or joining trading communities can provide support and motivation, reducing the emotional burden of trading alone.

Despite all these measures, emotional trading can still occur. When it does, be kind to yourself. Understand that it's a normal part of the trading journey. What matters is how quickly you recognize and address it. Continuous education and self-reflection are vital to improving your emotional discipline over time.

To sum up, while emotional trading is one of the most challenging aspects of Forex trading, it can be managed. Awareness, a solid trading plan, journaling, risk management, and cultivating the right mindset all contribute to a more disciplined approach. By taking proactive steps, you can minimize the influence of emotions and make more rational, profitable trading decisions.

The Role of Confidence and Patience

In the realm of Forex trading, confidence and patience are often underestimated components that play a crucial role in a trader's success. Without these attributes, even the most sophisticated strategies and technical analyses can fall flat. Confidence is not about being overly optimistic or arrogant; it's about having a measured, grounded belief in your trading plan and your ability to execute it. Similarly, patience is not merely the ability to wait but to keep a good attitude while waiting. Let's delve into why these traits are indispensable and how you can cultivate them.

Confidence in trading starts with a solid understanding of your strategy. When you know the ins and outs of your trading plan, you are more likely to stick with it even during periods of volatility. This assurance stems from thorough back-testing and forward-testing your strategies. The more familiar you are with your trading system's performance, including its strengths and weaknesses, the more confident you will be in executing trades according to plan.

Confidence is not static; it can be built and eroded over time. One way to build confidence is by setting small, achievable goals that provide quick wins. These small victories act as stepping stones, gradually building your confidence to handle larger trades and more complex scenarios. On the flip side, overconfidence can be dangerous. It can lead to taking unnecessary risks and deviating from your plan. Thus, it's vital to maintain a balanced view of your trading abilities.

Patience, on the other hand, is about timing and learning to wait for the right opportunities. Many traders fail because they lack the patience to wait for the ideal setup, entering trades prematurely. An excellent entry point can make the difference between a winning and a losing trade. Learning to wait for these high-probability setups is critical.

Building patience can be challenging in the fast-paced environment of Forex trading. One effective method is to implement checklists and predefined criteria for entering and exiting trades. By sticking to these checklists, you eliminate the impulsive decisions that can arise from emotional trading. Establishing a routine that includes regular breaks can also help you maintain focus and discipline, making it easier to wait for the right market conditions.

It's equally important to understand that patience is not just about waiting for entry points but also about letting your trades mature. Often, traders exit trades too early, either out of fear of losing profits or due to a lack of confidence in their analysis. Trusting your trade and having the patience to see it through to your predetermined exit point is essential for maximizing profits.

An excellent way to cultivate both confidence and patience is by maintaining a trading journal. Documenting each trade helps you review your performance objectively. Over time, you'll notice patterns—what works, what doesn't, and why. This reflection allows you to build confidence in your trading decisions and develop the patience to stick to your plan. A well-maintained journal becomes an invaluable tool for continuous improvement.

Market conditions can test even the most seasoned traders. During these times, the importance of confidence and patience becomes even more evident. Confidence helps you stay grounded, while patience allows you to avoid hasty decisions. Together, these traits enable you to navigate through periods of high volatility calmly and make reasoned decisions.

Mindfulness and mental conditioning exercises can be beneficial for enhancing your trading mindset. Techniques such as meditation, breathing exercises, and visualization can help maintain emotional equilibrium. When you're calm and focused, you're less likely to make impulsive decisions and more likely to stick to your trading plan. These exercises can act as a mental reset button, helping you approach trading with renewed confidence and patience.

Contrary to popular belief, confidence and patience are not innate qualities; they can be cultivated. Start by educating yourself thoroughly about the Forex market and your chosen trading strategies. Practice extensively in a demo environment before risking real capital. Gradually, you'll build the confidence needed to execute your plans and the patience to wait for the perfect trading opportunities.

In conclusion, confidence and patience are the unsung heroes of successful trading. They underpin your ability to execute strategies effectively and navigate market volatility. By focusing on self-improvement and continuously refining your approach to the market, you can build and sustain these essential traits, laying a solid foundation for long-term trading success.

Developing a Trader's Mindset

Becoming a successful Forex trader isn't just about mastering the technicalities of the market. While knowing your charts, indicators, and economic influences is crucial, equally important is cultivating a mindset attuned for trading. A trader's mindset is an amalgamation of psychological resilience, emotional intelligence, and strategic thinking. Ever wondered why some traders consistently succeed while others fail? It often boils down to their mental approach to trading.

One of the key aspects of a robust trader's mindset is understanding and embracing the inherent uncertainty of the market. Unlike other endeavors where more effort almost always translates to better results, the financial markets operate under their own set of rules. Accepting unpredictability can save you from overconfidence, a perilous emotional state that often precedes loss. Instead of seeking certainty, focus on probabilistic thinking. Ask yourself: What's the likelihood of this trade going my way?

Patience is more than just a virtue in trading—it's a necessity. There will be days when the market seems immobile, not offering any clear trading opportunities. On such occasions, impatience can drive you to make impulsive, sub-optimal decisions. The mindset of a disciplined trader involves waiting for the right setup based on your trading strategy, no matter how long it takes. Learn to find comfort in waiting, knowing that a hurried decision often leads to regrettable outcomes.

Moreover, confidence is important but must be balanced with humility. Confidence allows you to pull the trigger on trades without hesitation, trusting in your analysis and strategy. Humility ensures you recognize that every trade is a learning opportunity, and that you could be wrong. This balance enables you to take risks while remaining aware and cautious, avoiding the pitfalls of both overconfidence and fear.

Dealing with losses is another critical component of developing a trader's mindset. Losses are inevitable, but how you handle them makes all the difference. Embrace losses as part of the trading journey. Every loss is an opportunity for introspection and growth. Instead of viewing a losing trade as a failure, consider it an investment in your trading education. Reflect on what went wrong and what you could have done differently. This habit of constant learning will refine your strategy and mitigate future losses.

Emotional regulation can't be overstated. The market will test your emotional fortitude daily. Excitement, fear, greed, and frustration can cloud your judgment and lead to poor decision-making. Practice emotional regulation techniques like mindfulness and deep breathing. Establish routines that help ease your emotional state, ensuring you approach each trading session with a clear, focused mind. Remember that detached, rational decision-making often yields the best results.

Another aspect to consider is the ability to adapt and evolve. Financial markets are fluid and ever-changing. A trader's mindset must be adaptable, willing to alter strategies based on emerging trends and new information. Avoid becoming rigid in your approach. Flexibility and willingness to adjust can keep you ahead of the curve, maximizing your profitability.

Compartmentalization can also be beneficial in maintaining a balanced trading psyche. Don't let a bad trading day spill into your personal life. Learn to separate the trading world from your private life to ensure that one bad day doesn't exacerbate into something larger. This separation helps in maintaining a positive outlook and a refreshed mind for the next trading day.

Lastly, setting realistic expectations and goals is paramount. Unrealistic goals can lead to unnecessary pressure and stress, which can cloud judgment and prompt rash decisions. Focus on achievable, short-term targets while keeping an eye on your long-term growth. Instead of aiming to double your account in a week, aim for steady, incremental gains. This approach promotes sustainability and longevity in your trading career.

In conclusion, developing a trader's mindset is a multifaceted endeavor. It demands a blend of emotional resilience, strategic flexibility, and a constant thirst for learning. By embracing uncertainty, practicing patience, balancing confidence with humility, and continually refining your approach, you can foster a mindset that not only enhances your trading performance but also contributes to your overall growth as a trader. Remember, the market is as much a test of your psychology as it is of your analytical skills. Master both, and you're well on your way to becoming a consistently profitable trader.

Chapter 8: Developing a Comprehensive Trading Plan

In this chapter, we'll delve into the crucial elements of crafting a holistic and effective trading plan tailored to your individual needs as an intermediate to advanced Forex trader. Your plan should start with setting realistic trading objectives that align with your overall financial goals, ensuring they're specific, measurable, achievable, relevant, and time-bound. Next, establishing precise entry and exit rules helps to mitigate impulsive decisions, enhancing discipline and consistency in your trading practices. Equally vital is maintaining meticulous records of all your trades. By regularly reviewing these records, you can identify patterns and refine strategies, ultimately driving your trading efficiency and profitability. This chapter aims to guide you in structuring a comprehensive blueprint, setting you on a clear path to sustained success in the Forex market.

Setting Realistic Trading Objectives

In the world of Forex trading, the importance of setting realistic trading objectives can't be understated. Your objectives serve as a roadmap, guiding your daily decisions and long-term strategies. Without clear, attainable goals, your trading journey might resemble a ship lost at sea, drifting aimlessly with the current. The first step toward crafting these objectives is understanding what "realistic" means for your specific trading circumstances.

New traders often fall into the trap of setting overly ambitious goals, such as doubling their account every month. While optimism is valuable, unattainable targets can lead to reckless trading behavior and significant losses. To avoid this, utilize the SMART criteria—Specific, Measurable, Achievable, Relevant, and Time-bound—when defining your objectives. For instance, rather than aiming to "make a lot of money," aim to achieve a 5% return on your account over the next quarter.

Being specific about your financial goals enables you to design a tailored strategy. Start by asking yourself: What kind of trader are you? Long-term or short-term? Do you prefer day trading, swing trading, or position trading? Your trading style will significantly influence your objectives. A day trader might aim for frequent, small gains, while a swing trader might look for more substantial gains over a longer period. Aligning your goals with your trading style will make them more attainable.

Equally important is the need to measure your progress. As Peter Drucker famously said, "What gets measured, gets managed." Regularly track your trading performance against your set objectives. Are you hitting your targets most of the time? If not, it might be time to reassess your strategy and make necessary adjustments. Incorporate metrics like win rate, average profit per trade, and risk-reward ratio into your performance review. These metrics provide actionable insights and help you fine-tune your approach.

Setting achievable goals is perhaps the cornerstone of realistic objectives. It's one thing to aim high, but your goals should stretch your capabilities without breaking them. Unrealistic expectations can lead to frustration and irrational decisions, which are detrimental to your long-term success. If you're new to Forex trading, start with modest goals and scale up as your experience and confidence grow. For example, rather than targeting a $10,000 monthly profit from a $1,000 account, a more attainable goal might be a consistent monthly profit of 2-3%.

Relevance is another crucial factor. Your objectives should align with your overall financial goals and personal circumstances. Are you trading to supplement your income, or are you aiming for financial independence? Understanding your 'why' can provide clarity and purpose, making it easier to stick to your plan and resist the temptation of impulsive trades. Reflect on why you started trading in the first place and ensure that your goals align with this motivation.

The time-bound aspect of your objectives keeps you accountable. Assign specific time frames to your goals, whether they are daily, weekly, monthly, or yearly. A time-bound objective creates a sense of urgency and aids in tracking progress. For instance, a short-term goal might be to execute trades following all your entry and exit rules for a week. A long-term goal may involve achieving a certain return by the end of the year.

Your trading journey will inevitably involve both successes and setbacks. It's essential to maintain flexibility and adapt your objectives as you gain more experience. A fixed mindset will limit your growth. Instead, consider your objectives as evolving targets that can be adjusted based on market conditions, your personal life, and your trading performance. For example, if you find that achieving a 10% annual return is consistently manageable, consider raising your target to 12% or 15% while maintaining a prudent risk management approach.

Financial goals aren't the only type of objectives you should set. Skill-development goals can be equally valuable. For instance, mastering a particular technical indicator, improving your ability to interpret economic data, or learning new trading strategies can all be valid objectives. These goals often lead to long-term improvements in your trading performance. By focusing not only on the financial outcomes but also on skill enhancement, you build a more robust foundation for sustainable trading success.

Another critical aspect of setting realistic objectives is incorporating risk management. All too often, traders focus exclusively on potential profits without adequately considering the risks involved. Balance your financial goals with corresponding risk management rules. Define how much of your capital you're willing to risk on any single trade, and stick to that limit religiously. Consider objectives related to drawdowns as well. For example, aim to keep your maximum drawdown under 10% over a six-month period.

Engage in continuous learning and be open to feedback. Markets evolve, and so should your trading practices. Participate in trading forums, read industry publications, and possibly work with a mentor. Incorporating external perspectives can provide new insights that help refine your goals. This proactive approach to learning will ensure that your objectives remain relevant and attainable.

Finally, remember that no plan is set in stone. Periodically review and revise your objectives based on your trading performance, market conditions, and personal circumstances. Maintaining a flexible yet disciplined approach will help you stay on course toward your long-term trading success. Re-evaluating your goals isn't a sign of failure; it signifies adaptability and growth, which are essential traits of successful traders.

Having realistic trading objectives isn't just about setting targets for profits—it's about setting yourself up for sustainable success. Understand the "why" behind your trading goals, align them with your trading style, and measure your progress regularly. Balance your financial goals with skill-development objectives and integrate robust risk management into your plan. By doing so, you will create a comprehensive, realistic roadmap that paves the way for long-term profitability and trading mastery.

Entry and Exit Rules

In the landscape of Forex trading, one of the fundamental yet intricate components of a comprehensive trading plan is establishing clear entry and exit rules. These guidelines act as the backbone of your trading strategy, dictating when to open and close trades based on pre-determined criteria. By having well-defined entry and exit rules, traders can mitigate emotional decision-making and enhance overall consistency and profitability.

First, let's focus on entry rules. Establishing when to enter a trade is a critical decision that requires meticulous consideration of multiple factors. Traders often rely on technical indicators, chart patterns, and price action signals to inform these decisions. For example, a common entry strategy could involve waiting for a breakout above a resistance level, confirmed by an increase in trading volume. Alternatively, some traders prefer to enter trades based on specific technical indicators like the Moving Average Convergence Divergence (MACD) crossover or Relative Strength Index (RSI) levels.

Another effective method for setting entry rules is through the use of candlestick patterns. Candlestick patterns such as pin bars or engulfing patterns can provide timely entry signals when they occur at key support or resistance levels. These patterns often indicate potential price reversals or continuations, making them invaluable tools for timing entries. Additionally, combining multiple entry signals can improve the reliability of your trades. For instance, a trade signal might require both a bullish candlestick pattern and a confirmation from the MACD indicator to be considered valid.

While entry rules are crucial, having robust exit rules is equally, if not more important. Defining how and when to exit a trade allows traders to secure profits and limit losses, ultimately preserving their trading capital. There are several methodologies for establishing exit rules, including fixed targets, trailing stops, and dynamic exits based on market conditions.

Fixed targets involve setting a specific price level at which to exit the trade. This approach can be straightforward, but it requires careful analysis to ensure that the target is achievable given the market's volatility and trend. For instance, a trader might set a profit target at twice the risk taken on the trade. If the stop loss is placed at 50 pips, the profit target would be 100 pips. This helps maintain a favorable risk-to-reward ratio.

Trailing stops provide a more dynamic approach to exiting trades. Instead of setting a fixed target, a trailing stop moves in relation to the market price, locking in profits as the trade progresses favorably. For example, if a trader enters a long position and the price moves up, the trailing stop will follow the price at a set distance, say 20 pips, ensuring that the trader retains part of the profits even if the price later reverses. This technique can capture larger trends while still protecting gains.

Another strategy is to base exits on technical indicators. For instance, a trader might decide to exit a trade when the RSI enters overbought or oversold territory or when the MACD histogram shows a divergence. Such signals can suggest that the current trend is losing momentum, prompting an exit to safeguard profits or avoid potential losses.

Moreover, it is essential to integrate stop-loss orders into your exit rules. Stop-loss orders are pre-determined price levels where a trade will be automatically closed to prevent further losses. Implementing stop-loss orders ensures that traders adhere to their risk management strategies and protect their capital in volatile market conditions. A well-placed stop loss should be set based on technical levels rather than arbitrary figures. This could mean placing it just below a support level for long positions or above a resistance level for short positions.

Taking profit strategies are just as crucial. Some traders use a risk-to-reward ratio to determine their profit targets. For example, if a trader risks 1% of their account on a trade, they might aim for a 3% profit, giving a 1:3 risk-to-reward ratio. This helps ensure that the trader remains profitable over a series of trades, even if some trades result in losses.

Incorporating multiple exit strategies can significantly enhance your trading plan. For example, a partial exit strategy might involve closing out a portion of the trade at a pre-determined level and letting the rest ride the trend with a tightened trailing stop. This approach allows traders to secure some profits while staying in the market to capitalize on extended moves.

A key consideration in both entry and exit rules is flexibility. While having a strict set of guidelines is important, market conditions can change rapidly, and being able to adapt your strategy is crucial. This doesn't mean abandoning your rules entirely but rather having contingency plans or conditions under which you might alter your approach. For example, in highly volatile conditions, you might widen your stop losses and targets to accommodate greater price swings.

Moreover, it is essential to document and review your entry and exit rules consistently. Keeping detailed trade journals that record why trades were taken, the criteria met, and the outcome will help identify patterns and areas for improvement. Regular review sessions can provide valuable insights into the effectiveness of your trading plan and help refine your rules over time. Such reviews should not only focus on individual trades but also on the overall performance across multiple trades.

Also, incorporating backtesting into your strategy development can provide a reliable way to test your entry and exit rules against historical data. By simulating trades based on past market conditions, you can assess the viability of your rules without risking real capital.

This step requires thoroughness and honesty, as curve fitting—tweaking rules to fit historical data perfectly—can lead to poor real-world performance.

Finally, the psychological component of adhering to your entry and exit rules cannot be overstated. Discipline in following your predefined rules helps mitigate the emotional impulses that can lead to inconsistent and detrimental trading behavior. Friends, mastering your emotions and sticking to your strategy—especially during periods of drawdowns or high profits—is a hallmark of a successful trader.

In closing, having well-defined entry and exit rules is a cornerstone of a comprehensive Forex trading plan. These rules not only provide a roadmap for executing trades but also instill discipline and consistency, essential elements for long-term success in the Forex market. By meticulously planning and continuously refining these rules, traders can navigate the complexities of Forex trading with a structured approach that enhances profitability and mitigates risk.

Record Keeping and Review

Record keeping and review form the backbone of any comprehensive trading plan. It's essential to meticulously document every trade you make, highlighting the reasons behind them, the circumstances under which they were executed, and the results achieved. This practice is not merely about maintaining a tidy ledger; it's about creating a historical repository that aids in learning and continuous improvement.

A well-maintained trading journal is an indispensable tool for any serious trader. It offers a detailed record of trading activities, enabling you to identify patterns and trends in your behavior and the market. Each entry should include the date and time of the trade, the currency pair, the position size, entry and exit points, the strategy employed, and the outcomes. More importantly, jot down your thoughts and emotions at the time of the trade. Were you confident, anxious, or impulsive? These emotional cues can be significant indicators of future success or failure in your trades.

Consider this: If you don't document your trades, how can you expect to learn from your mistakes or replicate your successes? Documentation provides the raw data from which patterns emerge and from which lessons can be drawn. It's through these records that you'll begin to understand why some trades worked and others didn't. This retrospective analysis is paramount if you aim to refine your strategy continually.

After you've accumulated a substantial number of entries, it's time to dive into the review process. Regular reviews should be scheduled weekly, monthly, and quarterly. Each review period serves a different purpose and provides varied insights.

During your weekly reviews, focus on the short-term. Examine the week's trades with an eagle eye, discerning what went well and identifying immediate areas for improvement. Were there any unexpected market behaviors this week? Did you overtrade or miss promising setups? The answers to these questions will help you tweak your strategy for the upcoming week.

Monthly reviews, on the other hand, should focus more on the medium-term view. Here, you'll aggregate data from the weekly reviews to identify broad trends. Are there recurring mistakes? Are you consistently falling short of your targets, or are you exceeding them? This level of review allows for more substantial changes to your trading plan if needed. For instance, if you consistently notice that certain market conditions lead to losses, you might decide to avoid trading during such times.

Then there are the quarterly reviews, your long-term analysis sessions. These reviews are about evaluating the overall effectiveness of your trading strategy. Compare your performance with the goals you set at the beginning of the quarter. Are you on track? If not, why not? This high-level overview is crucial for strategic adjustments, potentially even a reevaluation of your trading approach or objectives. Perhaps you need to change your trading style or incorporate new indicators.

Another invaluable benefit of structured record keeping is it lays the foundation for backtesting and forward testing future strategies. By having a rich historical dataset, you're better positioned to test new approaches under various market conditions. When you back-test, you simulate how a strategy would have performed in the past, using your real historical data to verify its accuracy. While backtesting alone isn't foolproof, when combined with forward testing—where you apply the strategy in current market conditions before committing real capital—it becomes extraordinarily powerful.

It's also worth mentioning that meticulous record keeping can enhance your discipline. Knowing that you'll have to write down the details of every trade can serve as a deterrent against impulsive decisions. In a sense, it conditions you to follow your trading plan more rigorously, fostering a habit of accountability that's crucial for long-term success.

While technology has made the record-keeping process more straightforward, the principles behind it remain the same. Numerous software solutions are available that can automatically log trades and generate analytical reports. However, even with these tools, manual input—especially regarding your emotional state and decision-making rationale—can provide insights that automated systems miss. Use technology as an aid, not a crutch.

Aside from the numbers and statistics, consider including screenshots of charts at the time of each trade in your journal. Visual references can be incredibly insightful, allowing you to see the market context that numbers alone can't convey. These images can highlight whether you correctly identified patterns and trends or if there were biases clouding your judgment.

Moreover, a trading journal can be a motivational tool. Tracking your progress over time shows how far you've come, providing tangible proof of your learning curve and growth as a trader. Periodically review your earliest entries and compare them with your most recent ones. The differences will likely be stark, underscoring your development and the efficacy of a comprehensive record-keeping system.

Lastly, no trader is an island. Sharing your trading journal with a mentor or a trading community can provide external perspectives that can be incredibly valuable. Others might spot patterns or biases you've overlooked, offering constructive feedback that can help refine your strategy. Just the act of sharing can inject a sense of accountability and commitment into your trading practice.

In conclusion, record keeping and review are not just aspects of a trading plan; they are foundations upon which the plan builds and evolves. Without this structured approach to tracking and analyzing your trades, you risk repeating mistakes and missing opportunities for growth. By making record-keeping and regular review integral components of your trading routine, you lay the groundwork for sustained improvement and, ultimately, greater profitability.

Chapter 9: Algorithmic Trading in Forex

Algorithmic trading has revolutionized Forex markets by leveraging computer programs to execute trades with precision and speed that humans can't match. This chapter dives into the core concepts that make algorithmic trading a powerful tool for both novice and seasoned traders. You'll learn how to develop and test your own trading algorithms, exploring the intricacies of coding these automated strategies to suit various market conditions. We'll weigh the pros and cons, dissecting the benefits like removing emotional bias and the risks such as over-optimization. By the end, you'll have a robust understanding of how to incorporate algorithmic trading into your existing strategies, thus enhancing your trading efficiency and effectiveness.

Introduction to Algorithmic Trading

Algorithmic trading, often referred to as "algo trading" or "automated trading," has revolutionized the world of forex trading by leveraging the power of advanced computing and data analysis. This section aims to introduce the foundational concepts of algorithmic trading, providing you with a comprehensive understanding of how algorithms can enhance your forex trading strategies and improve your overall trading performance.

At its core, algorithmic trading uses pre-programmed instructions to execute trades at speeds and frequencies that are impossible for a human trader. These instructions, or "algorithms," use a variety of quantitative models to make decisions based on market data. The primary objective is to spot trading opportunities that offer the best risk/reward ratios while minimizing human error and emotional decision-making.

The first advantage of algorithmic trading is its ability to process vast amounts of data in real-time. An algorithm can analyze historical and live market data to identify patterns, calculate technical indicators, and execute trades based on predefined criteria—all within fractions of a second. This allows traders to exploit market inefficiencies and capitalize on price movements more efficiently than traditional manual methods.

Another benefit is the potential for improved execution quality. Algorithms can minimize slippage by executing orders at optimal prices and reducing the market impact of large trades. Automated systems can break down a large order into smaller, more manageable chunks and execute them over time, thus avoiding the pitfalls of revealing the trader's intentions to the broader market.

The role of algorithmic trading extends beyond execution to include strategy development and backtesting. Traders can develop sophisticated trading strategies that incorporate multiple indicators, statistical models, and machine learning algorithms. These strategies can be rigorously tested on historical data to evaluate their performance and refine the trading rules before deploying them in live markets. Backtesting provides invaluable insights into a strategy's robustness and helps traders anticipate how it might perform under different market conditions.

Despite its numerous advantages, algorithmic trading is not without challenges. Developing an effective trading algorithm requires a deep understanding of both trading principles and programming skills. Traders must be proficient in languages like Python, R, or C++ to code the algorithms. Additionally, maintaining an algorithmic trading system requires constant monitoring and adjustments to reflect changes in market conditions and to address potential bugs or algorithmic failures.

A pivotal component of algorithmic trading is the concept of "high-frequency trading" (HFT). High-frequency trading is a subset of algorithmic trading characterized by the high speed at which trades are executed—often in microseconds. HFT strategies capitalize on very short-term market inefficiencies and require substantial computational power and low-latency data feeds to be successful.

Transitioning to algo trading also involves substantial infrastructure investment. Setting up a reliable algorithmic trading system requires robust hardware, advanced software, and secure network connections. Traders need access to high-quality data feeds and trading APIs provided by brokers, as well as backup systems to ensure operations remain uninterrupted during technical issues.

Moreover, risk management remains a critical aspect of algo trading. Algorithms must be designed to manage risk effectively, incorporating features like stop-loss limits, position sizing rules, and risk thresholds to protect against catastrophic losses. It's essential to have safeguards in place to halt trading activities if the algorithm behaves unexpectedly or market conditions become extreme.

Ethical considerations also come into play. High-frequency traders, in particular, have faced scrutiny for potentially creating market volatility and benefiting at the expense of slower market participants. Regulatory bodies worldwide are increasingly monitoring algorithmic trading practices to ensure market fairness and integrity. Compliance with these regulations is mandatory, and failure to adhere can result in severe penalties.

Lastly, the journey into algorithmic trading should begin with a thorough education. Books, online courses, seminars, and forums provide valuable resources that can help traders build their knowledge and coding skills. Collaborating with other traders and developers can also speed up the learning process and offer new perspectives on strategy development.

In summary, algorithmic trading represents a powerful tool for modern forex traders, combining the strengths of computational power and quantitative analysis to create more efficient, consistent, and profitable trading strategies. However, it requires a significant investment of time and resources to develop, implement, and maintain. Done correctly, the rewards can be substantial, offering traders a cutting-edge approach to navigating the complexities of the forex market while managing risks effectively.

Building and Testing Trading Algorithms

Building a trading algorithm begins with a solid understanding of the market you're trading in. For Forex traders, knowledge of currency pairs, market hours, volatility, and economic indicators is essential. However, beyond the foundational knowledge, algorithmic trading requires a methodical approach to coding and testing strategies.

First, you'll need to identify the strategy that you want to automate. This strategy should be based on well-researched principles and tested through manual trading or backtesting. Once identified, the key is to define clear entry and exit points. For example, you may use moving averages to detect trends or look for price action patterns like pin bars and inside bars. This clear outline helps you translate these conditions into code.

Breaking down the components of your strategy is crucial. You need to translate each element of your trading rules into programmable steps. This includes setting up conditions for entering a trade, the criteria for exiting, stop-loss levels, and take-profit targets. Depending on your coding skills, you might use languages like Python, MQL4/5 for MetaTrader, or even more advanced platforms like TradeStation.

Financial data cleaning and preprocessing are necessary steps before you start coding the algorithm. Ensure you have high-quality and accurate historical data. Gaps in data or inaccuracies can yield misleading results. Data libraries such as pandas in Python are particularly useful for managing and manipulating historical data.

Now, the coding begins. You'd start by defining key variables—such as the length of moving averages, look-back periods for indicators, and thresholds for trade entries and exits. Keep your code modular; break down different parts of your strategy into functions that can be individually tested and debugged. This makes updating or altering the strategy far easier.

Backtesting is the next critical step. Backtesting involves running your strategy against historical data to see how it would have performed. Be mindful of "look-ahead bias," where the algorithm inadvertently uses data not available at the time of the trade. Use dedicated libraries like backtrader in Python to facilitate this process. Backtesting platforms often provide performance metrics such as return on investment, drawdown, and winning percentage, helping you evaluate the efficacy of your strategy.

Optimization emerges as a key aspect after initial backtesting. This involves tweaking various parameters to achieve the highest returns or minimal drawdowns. Use caution here, as over-optimization can lead to "curve-fitting," where your algorithm excels on historical data but performs poorly in live markets. Split your data into in-sample and out-of-sample sets to validate the robustness of your strategy across different time periods.

After you've thoroughly backtested and optimized your algorithm, it's time for forward testing. Also known as paper trading, forward testing involves running your algorithm in a live market environment but without risking actual capital. This simulation lets you observe how the strategy performs under current market conditions, providing another layer of validation. Platforms like MetaTrader offer demo accounts where you can execute forward tests effectively.

Risk management must never be neglected in algorithmic trading. Incorporate mechanisms like stop-loss and take-profit levels right into your code. Position sizing is another critical element; algorithms can manage position sizes based on account equity or predefined risk levels. Proper risk management ensures that your strategy can withstand market downturns.

Once satisfied with forward testing, you may opt for deploying your algorithm in a live market. Start small, perhaps using micro or mini lots, before scaling up. Regularly review performance to ensure the algorithm is trading as expected. Keep an eye on regulatory changes and market conditions that could impact your strategy.

Remember, trading algorithms aren't set-and-forget tools. They require ongoing monitoring and adjustments to adapt to changing market dynamics. Regularly update your algorithm to incorporate new insights and improvements. Continue learning, whether it's through further financial education or upgrading your coding skills.

With algorithmic trading, the journey from concept to implementation involves multiple stages of strategy development, rigorous testing, and risk management. Each step contributes to building a robust, profitable trading algorithm that can potentially enhance your Forex trading success.

Pros and Cons of Automated Trading

Algorithmic trading, or automated trading, has become a fixture in modern Forex markets. Its allure lies in its ability to execute trades at lightning speed, sometimes in milliseconds, and its capacity to process vast amounts of market data ceaselessly. However, like any sophisticated tool, automated trading is a double-edged sword, endowed with both compelling advantages and inherent drawbacks. This section delves into the salient pros and cons of relying on automated trading systems in the high-stakes arena of Forex trading.

Pros of Automated Trading

First and foremost, automated trading systems eliminate the emotional influences that often compromise the decision-making processes of human traders. Emotions like fear and greed can wreak havoc on trading strategies, causing traders to deviate from their planned course of action. By using automated systems, trades are executed based on pre-defined algorithms, free from emotional pitfalls.

The speed and efficiency of automated trading are unrivaled. These systems can analyze multiple markets and instruments simultaneously, providing traders with the ability to exploit opportunities that would be impossible to track manually. In high-frequency trading, where milliseconds can mean the difference between profit and loss, the speed of automated systems offers a formidable advantage.

Another major pro is consistency. Automated trading ensures that trading rules and strategies are applied consistently, which is particularly crucial in complex scenarios where human judgment might falter. Consistency helps maintain disciplined trading and adherence to a well-defined strategy, these elements are essential for long-term success.

Scalability is also an important advantage. Once a trading strategy is formulated and tested, scaling it up to handle larger volumes or multiple currency pairs is relatively straightforward. Automated systems can handle thousands of trades per day, something that would be humanly impossible to achieve manually.

Additionally, automated trading allows for backtesting. This involves running trading strategies on historical data to assess their viability before deploying them in real-time markets. Backtesting provides valuable insights into the effectiveness and potential profitability of a strategy, allowing traders to fine-tune and iterate before taking on live market risk.

Cons of Automated Trading

While the benefits are compelling, automated trading is not without its drawbacks. Perhaps the most significant risk is over-optimization, also known as curve-fitting. This occurs when a strategy is too finely tuned to historical data, making it less effective in real-world, unpredictable market conditions. Over-optimized models often perform spectacularly in backtests, but fail to deliver similar results in live trading due to their lack of robustness.

Technical issues present another serious concern. Automated trading systems rely heavily on technology, including software, hardware, and stable internet connections. A minor glitch or latency issue can lead to erroneous trades with potentially catastrophic financial consequences. There's also the risk of system failures or bugs, which can cause significant financial loss if not immediately addressed.

Furthermore, automated systems lack the adaptability and critical thinking abilities that human traders bring to the table. While an algorithm can follow pre-set rules, it cannot adjust to unforeseen events or market anomalies without human intervention. This lack of adaptability can be a severe disadvantage in volatile or unprecedented market conditions.

Cost is another factor to consider. Developing or purchasing an automated trading system can be expensive. Moreover, the costs don't end there. Maintaining and continuously updating the system requires financial resources and technical expertise. Subscription fees for data feeds and trading platforms can further add to the overhead.

Another concern is the potential for market abuse and manipulation. High-frequency trading algorithms can execute a large number of trades in a short time, potentially creating artificial volatility or manipulating price levels. While regulatory bodies are continually evolving to curb such practices, the potential for misuse remains a risk inherent in highly automated trading environments.

Moreover, regulatory scrutiny is intensifying. Trading algorithms must comply with various regulations, which can vary by jurisdiction. Non-compliance can result in hefty fines and legal repercussions. Traders must ensure that their algorithms not only perform well but also adhere to regulatory guidelines.

Balancing Automation and Human Expertise

Given these pros and cons, it becomes clear that while automated trading can significantly enhance trading efficiency and profitability, it should not be viewed as a panacea. Human oversight is indispensable for addressing the shortcomings of algorithmic systems. Successful traders often employ a hybrid approach, leveraging the speed and consistency of automated systems while retaining the adaptability and critical thinking capacities of human judgment.

In practice, this might mean using automated systems for specific tasks, such as executing trades or monitoring market conditions, while retaining aspects like strategy formulation, risk management, and adaptive decision-making for human traders. Combining the strengths of both human and machine can create a more robust and adaptable trading strategy, capable of navigating the complexities of Forex markets.

Moreover, it's crucial for traders to continually educate themselves and stay updated on technological advancements. Understanding how algorithms work and regularly reviewing and updating trading systems can mitigate many of the risks associated with automated trading. Continuous learning and adaptation are key in leveraging the full potential of automated trading while minimizing its downsides.

Ultimately, the decision to integrate automated trading into your Forex strategy should be contingent on a thorough understanding of its advantages and limitations. By balancing automation with human expertise, traders can position themselves to capitalize on the benefits of algorithmic trading while safeguarding against its inherent risks.

Chapter 10: Advanced Strategies in Action

In this chapter, we dive deep into sophisticated strategies that take your Forex trading to the next level, focusing on the practical application of Scalping, Day Trading vs. Swing Trading, and the Carry Trade strategy. Scalping strategies require precision and quick decision-making to capture small price movements, demanding focus and agility. Contrastingly, Day Trading and Swing Trading provide more flexibility—Day Trading involves making multiple trades within a single day, while Swing Trading spans several days to weeks to capture larger price shifts. The Carry Trade strategy leverages interest rate differentials between currencies to generate profit, necessitating a thorough understanding of economic fundamentals and risk management. By mastering these advanced strategies, you can significantly enhance your trading efficacy and profitability. Whether you're aiming for rapid gains or gradual growth, these techniques offer versatile tools for varied market conditions and personal trading styles.

Scalping Strategies

Scalping, as a trading strategy, requires a refined skill set and an imperturbable focus. For intermediate and advanced Forex traders, it can be a lucrative way to capitalize on minor price movements within the trading day. This method relies on executing high volumes of trades for small profits. Although the profit per trade might be meager, the cumulative gains can be significant for those who master the intricacies.

Scalping demands a deep understanding of market dynamics and razor-sharp precision. The most successful scalpers employ advanced techniques that allow them to navigate market volatility with confidence. The key here is speed and efficiency—in both decision-making and execution.

A quintessential part of scalping is the quick identification of entry and exit points. Traders use a variety of tools, such as real-time charts, technical indicators, and advanced analytics, to pinpoint these opportunities. You must be adept at reading short-term patterns and reacting swiftly to market changes.

One common approach in scalping is prioritizing highly liquid currency pairs like EUR/USD, GBP/USD, and USD/JPY. The high liquidity ensures tight spreads, which is crucial for a strategy that relies on small margins. Scalpers also need to be aware of the most active trading hours, usually when major markets overlap, to take full advantage of the volatility and volume.

Different scalpers employ various strategies, often customized to their comfort level and trading style. Some prefer to use time-based strategies, exploiting specific hours of the trading day when volatility is highest. Others might focus on a high-frequency trading model where the sheer number of trades compensates for the modest profit per trade. The latter often necessitates an algorithmic approach due to the speed required.

Risk management in scalping poses its own set of challenges. Given the nature of this strategy, the potential for losses can be just as rapid as the potential for gains. Traders must employ strict stop-loss orders and keep a close watch on the market to prevent significant losses. This vigilance helps in maintaining a favorable risk-to-reward ratio, even when individual trade profits are minimal.

Advanced charting tools are invaluable for scalpers. Patterns such as flags, triangles, and channels can provide predictive insights for imminent market movements. When combined with stochastic oscillators or other momentum indicators, these patterns can enhance the accuracy of predicting price actions.

Another critical aspect is managing transaction costs. Frequent trades can rack up substantial fees, which can eat into profits. Scalpers need to minimize costs by using brokers with low spreads and commissions. It's also important to be aware of any hidden fees that could impact overall profitability.

Scalping requires an almost obsessive attention to detail and the ability to thrive under pressure. Its success hinges on consistently making small profits and avoiding large losses. The mental agility needed for this strategy cannot be overstated; traders must be emotionally resilient and capable of maintaining focus in the face of rapid market movements.

For those willing to invest in sophisticated technology, algorithmic trading systems offer a significant advantage. These systems can execute trades at lightning speed, adhering strictly to pre-set parameters and eliminating the delay caused by human decision-making. However, algorithm development requires a profound understanding of both coding and market dynamics, making it suitable primarily for those with a technical background.

Filter strategies often come into play in scalping. For instance, some traders use volume filters to identify trades where trading volume validates the directional move, thus ensuring that every trade capitalizes on strong market interest. This minimizes the risk associated with false breakouts and provides additional layers of confirmation before executing a trade.

Traders also frequently employ techniques like price laddering. This involves placing trades at multiple levels both above and below the market price, creating a sort of safety net if the price doesn't move as anticipated. It requires more complex risk management but can significantly smooth out the profit curve over time.

Speed is one of the defining elements of scalping. Automated systems and hotkeys are often used to ensure that trades are executed almost instantaneously. This precision is critical in volatile markets where delays of even a few seconds can mean the difference between profit and loss.

Experienced scalpers develop an intuitive feel for the market over time. This instinct, combined with a robust strategy, can differentiate between a successful scalper and one who struggles. Building this intuition requires practice, continuous learning, and constant market engagement.

Lastly, it's essential to review and adapt your scalping strategies continuously. The Forex market is dynamic, and what works today might not be as effective tomorrow. Regularly analyzing performance metrics, refining techniques, and staying updated with market news and trends can keep your scalping strategies in top shape.

Day Trading vs. Swing Trading Strategies

In the vast realm of forex trading, two popular strategies often come under scrutiny: Day Trading and Swing Trading. While both strategies offer avenues to profitability, their approach, time commitments, and risk profiles can significantly differ. Understanding these nuances is crucial for traders aiming to refine their strategies and optimize returns.

Day trading, as the name suggests, involves making trades within a single trading day. Day traders capitalize on short-term price movements. This strategy requires traders to be glued to their screens, monitoring currency pairs with a laser focus. They aim to exploit small price fluctuations and often leverage higher positions to maximize gains. A typical day trader might make several trades a day, each targeting minute price variances.

On the flip side, swing trading operates on a broader time horizon. Swing traders seek to capture price swings over several days, or even weeks. They rely heavily on technical analysis, chart patterns, and sometimes fundamental analysis to predict medium-term market movements. Swing trading allows for more flexibility and does not necessitate constant monitoring, making it accessible for those who juggle trading with other commitments.

The instruments utilized by day traders and swing traders can also differ. Day traders might lean on shorter-term indicators such as the Relative Strength Index (RSI) or the Moving Average Convergence Divergence (MACD) for instant signals. They might also employ tactics like scalping, which involves profiting from small price changes repeatedly throughout the day.

Swing traders, however, often incorporate tools that identify broader trends, like support and resistance levels or longer-term moving averages. They look for technical patterns, like head and shoulders or double tops, which tend to signal more significant potential price moves. These patterns are instrumental in determining entry and exit points.

Risk management is another critical distinction between these trading strategies. Day trading, due to its rapid pace and frequent trades, involves handling a higher number of smaller risks. Day traders typically utilize tight stop-loss orders to prevent significant losses. They are constantly adjusting their positions to adapt to the market's swift changes.

Swing trading, conversely, carries the risk over a longer period, and hence, the potential drawdown per trade might be more substantial.

Swing traders set wider stop-loss levels to accommodate the broader price swings they are aiming to capture. Risk management in swing trading often involves balancing position sizes and utilizing trailing stops to lock in profits as positions move in their favor.

Psychologically, day trading demands a high level of focus, quick decision-making, and the ability to handle stress. The fast-paced nature can be overwhelming, and emotions like fear and greed can dramatically impact performance. Traders need to have a disciplined mindset and precise execution strategies.

Swing trading, while less intense, requires patience and confidence in one's analysis. The longer holding period means more exposure to market volatility and potential news-driven price movements. Consequently, traders must manage the psychological challenge of sticking to their plan despite short-term market fluctuations.

Both strategies have their advantages and disadvantages. Day trading offers quick returns and the excitement of rapid trading but demands extensive time and attention. It's suited for those who enjoy the thrill of the fast-paced trading environment and can dedicate their day to managing trades.

Swing trading, meanwhile, offers more substantial potential profits per trade and requires less screen time, providing flexibility. It's ideal for those who analyze markets thoroughly and can withstand holding positions over several days without reacting impulsively to every market movement.

Choosing between day trading and swing trading isn't merely about preference; it hinges on one's lifestyle, risk tolerance, and trading goals. Some traders may even combine elements of both strategies, depending on the market conditions and their individual plans.

By understanding the intricate dynamics of both day and swing trading, intermediate to advanced traders can better align their strategies with their personal goals and market outlook. This alignment, coupled with continuous learning and adaptation, is pivotal in navigating the forex market's complexities and achieving sustained profitability.

In the realm of forex, there's no one-size-fits-all strategy. Day and swing trading each offer unique pathways to success, and mastery of either (or both) can propel traders towards their financial goals. The key lies in understanding the principles behind each approach, solid risk management, and the psychological fortitude to stay disciplined and consistent.

Carry Trade Strategy

Among the myriad advanced strategies available to contemporary Forex traders, the carry trade strategy stands out due to its potential to deliver consistent returns over time. Unlike short-term maneuvers such as scalping or day trading, carry trade is a longer-term strategy that capitalizes on the differences in interest rates between two currencies. Simply put, it involves borrowing funds in a currency with a low-interest rate and investing them in a currency with a higher interest rate. The objective is to profit from the interest rate differentials, known as the "carry".

Carry trade strategies revolve around understanding and harnessing interest rate differentials. At its core, the strategy involves selling a currency with a relatively low interest rate and purchasing a currency boasting a higher interest rate. For instance, one might borrow Japanese Yen, which has historically low interest rates, to buy Australian Dollars, a currency known for its higher rates. The profit is derived from the interest rate differential between the two currencies, accruing interest as the trade is left open.

One of the main reasons carry trade strategies hold such appeal is their potential for double-digit annual returns, provided that market conditions remain favorable. However, it is crucial to recognize that carry trade is not without its risks. Unlike short-term trading strategies that can quickly adapt to market movements, carry trades are vulnerable to changes in interest rates and economic conditions, which can impact profitability.

Timing is essential when employing a carry trade strategy. Traders must thoroughly analyze the broader economic environment and central bank policies. A sudden change in interest rates or geopolitical events can sharply impact currency values, and therefore, the profitability of the trade. Understanding macroeconomic indicators is pivotal, as these often predict shifts in interest rates. For example, central banks adjusting rates to curtail inflation or stimulate economic growth can impact the performance of carry trades.

Consider the importance of leverage when executing carry trades. While leveraging can amplify returns, it concurrently magnifies risks. Traders must be diligent in managing leverage levels, ensuring they do not overextend and expose themselves to excessive risks. A carry trade might seem appealing due to potential returns; however, without appropriate risk management, traders may find themselves heavily impacted by adverse market movements. Position sizing and diversification are key risk management techniques in this regard.

Another critical aspect of carry trade strategies is the "rollover" process. In Forex trading, when a trader holds a position past the market close, they incur a rollover fee, which can be positive or negative depending on the interest rate differential between the two currencies. For carry trades, a positive rollover fee, known as the "carry yield," is desirable as it contributes to the overall profitability of the trade. Conversely, negative carry can incur costs, eroding the trade's profitability.

The strategic selection of currency pairs is fundamental to successful carry trades. High-yield currencies such as the New Zealand

Dollar (NZD) or Australian Dollar (AUD) are often paired with low-yielders like the Japanese Yen (JPY) or Swiss Franc (CHF). These pairings can offer attractive interest rate differentials. However, traders should not solely base their decisions on interest rate differentials but also consider factors such as market volatility and economic stability, which can influence currency performance.

Monitoring market sentiment is another critical facet of carry trade strategies. Positive sentiment and market confidence can bolster high-yield currencies, making the carry trade more profitable. Conversely, during periods of market uncertainty or risk aversion, traders might flee to safe-haven currencies, causing high-yield currencies to depreciate. Thus, keeping a pulse on global financial markets and investor sentiment is indispensable.

To mitigate risks associated with carry trades, traders can utilize stop-loss orders. By setting predefined exit points, traders can limit potential losses if the market moves unfavorably. Additionally, traders can employ technical analysis tools to identify trend directions and potential turning points, providing a more comprehensive view of the market dynamics.

It's also worth noting that carry trade strategies may not always yield consistent returns over the long term. Financial markets are inherently dynamic, and changes in interest rates, economic policies, and geopolitical events can alter the landscape. For instance, during economic downturns, central banks may reduce interest rates to stimulate growth, narrowing the interest rate differentials that carry trades rely on. Consequently, traders must remain adaptable, constantly reassessing their positions and adjusting their strategies based on evolving market conditions.

Furthermore, currency pair correlations should not be overlooked. Understanding how different currency pairs interact can help traders manage risk and diversify their portfolios. For instance, currency pairs that are positively correlated tend to move in the same direction, while negatively correlated pairs move in opposite directions. Hedging against these correlations can provide an additional layer of risk mitigation, ensuring that adverse movements in one currency pair do not significantly impact overall profitability.

The importance of comprehensive research and due diligence cannot be overstated when employing carry trade strategies. Traders must stay updated with economic reports, interest rate decisions, and geopolitical events that can impact currency values. Reliable Forex news sources, economic calendars, and analytical tools are indispensable resources that can assist traders in making informed decisions and enhancing the profitability of their carry trades.

In summary, carry trade strategies offer a compelling approach for Forex traders seeking to leverage interest rate differentials for consistent returns. However, this strategy is not without its complexities and risks. By thoroughly understanding the economic landscape, managing leverage and risk, monitoring market sentiment, and conducting diligent research, traders can effectively navigate the intricacies of carry trades and optimize their profitability in the ever-evolving Forex market.

Chapter 11: Mastering Divergence Trading

Divergence trading is a sophisticated technique that involves identifying discrepancies between the price of a currency pair and indicators like the Relative Strength Index (RSI) or Moving Average Convergence Divergence (MACD). Understanding these divergences can provide invaluable insights into potential trend reversals before they become evident to the broader market. By mastering both bullish and bearish divergences, you can anticipate market movements more accurately, placing you ahead of the curve. Integrating divergence trading with other strategies, such as support and resistance levels or price action patterns, can offer a multi-layered approach to refining your entries and exits. This chapter delves into these complexities, enabling you to harness the power of divergence to enhance your trading strategies and increase your profitability.

Identifying Divergences

Divergences are a crucial aspect of technical analysis in Forex trading, providing traders with insights that might be overlooked when relying solely on price movement. At its core, divergence indicates a discrepancy between the direction of price and the momentum of an indicator. This discrepancy often signals potential reversals or continuations in trend, making it a valuable tool for intermediate to advanced traders.

To identify divergences, it's essential to understand their two main types: regular (or classic) divergence and hidden divergence. Regular divergence is often used to predict potential trend reversals. When the price reaches new highs or lows, but the indicator doesn't, this disparity can suggest that the current trend is losing strength and might reverse.

Hidden divergence, on the other hand, is typically used to identify trend continuations. It occurs when the price forms a higher low in an uptrend or a lower high in a downtrend, but the indicator doesn't support this price movement. Recognizing hidden divergence can be critical for traders looking to join an established trend.

For identifying divergences, commonly used momentum indicators include the Relative Strength Index (RSI), Moving Average Convergence Divergence (MACD), and Stochastic Oscillator. Each of these indicators measures the speed and change of price movements, offering different perspectives on the market's momentum.

RSI is particularly popular among traders for spotting divergences. It oscillates between 0 and 100, with values above 70 indicating overbought conditions and below 30 suggesting oversold conditions. When the RSI shows opposite movement to the price, divergence is indicated. For example, if the price makes higher highs but the RSI forms lower highs, it signals bearish divergence, hinting at a potential downward reversal.

MACD is another powerful tool for detecting divergences. Comprising of two moving averages, the MACD line and the signal line, and a histogram, it helps traders visualize the momentum and trend strength. When the price forms higher highs and the MACD line forms lower highs, it shows bearish divergence. Conversely, price forming lower lows while the MACD creates higher lows implies bullish divergence, suggesting an upward reversal could be on the horizon.

Though not as frequently mentioned, the Stochastic Oscillator is equally effective for identifying divergences. It compares a particular closing price to a range of its prices over a certain period. When the Stochastic forms a pattern that's inconsistent with price movement, it often foretells a reversal or a continuation, depending on whether the divergence is regular or hidden.

You'll want to incorporate multiple indicators to confirm divergences and reduce the likelihood of false signals. An isolated divergence might not be reliable, but confirming it across different indicators adds strength to the hypothesis. For instance, a bearish divergence observed in both RSI and MACD is a stronger signal than seeing it in only one metric.

When identifying divergences, context is everything. It's crucial to consider the overall market trend and other factors, such as volume and support and resistance levels. Divergences are less reliable in choppy or sideways markets, where false signals can be frequent. They're particularly potent in trending markets where they can indicate the strength or weakness of the current trend.

Another vital aspect of recognizing divergences is the timeframe you're analyzing. Longer timeframes tend to provide more reliable signals but might result in delayed entries. Shorter timeframes can offer quicker signals but are more prone to noise and false divergences. A balanced approach might involve confirming a divergence seen on a shorter timeframe with the trend context on a longer timeframe.

Practical experience is key to mastering divergence identification. Spend time backtesting this concept on historical charts, using different timeframes and indicators. This hands-on approach helps you become familiar with how divergences manifest and how reliable they are in various market conditions.

Though backtesting is invaluable, live trading presents different challenges. Market conditions are constantly evolving, and the emotional pressure of managing real money can affect decision-making. Start by applying your divergence identification skills in a demo or paper trading account to build confidence and proficiency.

In conclusion, identifying divergences is a powerful skill that can significantly enhance your Forex trading strategy. By understanding the nuances of regular and hidden divergences, utilizing momentum indicators like RSI, MACD, and Stochastic Oscillator, and applying a multi-indicator confirmation approach, you can uncover valuable trading opportunities. Contextual awareness, practical experience, and thoughtful application across different market conditions will hone this skill further, contributing to your overall trading success.

Trading Bullish and Bearish Divergences

Divergence trading is a fundamental concept that allows traders to spot potential reversals in market trends by comparing price movements with technical indicators. It pinpoints moments when the market momentum diverges from the price action, indicating a possible shift. Understanding how to effectively trade bullish and bearish divergences can significantly elevate your trading prowess.

Bullish divergences occur when prices form lower lows while a technical indicator, such as the Relative Strength Index (RSI) or Moving Average Convergence Divergence (MACD), forms higher lows. This divergence signals that the downward momentum is weakening, and a price reversal to the upside could be imminent. In the same vein, bearish divergences take place when prices make higher highs, but the indicator records lower highs, signifying that the upward momentum is faltering and a potential reversal to the downside may be near.

To illustrate, let's consider a scenario involving the RSI. If you're observing a downtrend where the price charts show lower lows but the RSI begins to form higher lows, this bullish divergence can alert you to a possible upward trend reversal. Similarly, if you spot the price making higher highs during an uptrend while the RSI is making lower highs, this bearish divergence could warn you of an impending downtrend.

One effective approach to trading these divergences involves confirming them through multiple timeframes. By examining both shorter and longer timeframes, traders can validate the divergence's strength. For instance, a bullish divergence on a 4-hour chart confirmed by a similar pattern on the daily chart reinforces the likelihood of a legitimate reversal, increasing your confidence in executing trades.

Incorporating divergence trading into your overall strategy involves more than just identifying the setup. It's crucial to pair divergences with other technical tools like trend lines, support and resistance levels, and candlestick patterns. This multi-factor approach ensures that you're not relying solely on single indicators but rather a confluence of data points that collectively confirm a trading opportunity.

The key to effectively trading bullish and bearish divergences lies in proper risk management and strategic entry and exit points. When a divergence is identified and confirmed, a stop loss can be placed just below the recent low in the case of a bullish divergence or above the recent high for a bearish divergence. This strategy safeguards your position should the market move contrary to your analysis.

Additionally, while trading divergences can be lucrative, it's not without its pitfalls. False signals can and do occur, leading to potential losses. Therefore, ensuring that your trades have a robust risk-to-reward ratio is critical. Aiming for a minimum ratio of 2:1 can help manage risk effectively. This means your potential profit should be at least double your potential loss, providing a cushion in case the trade doesn't play out as expected.

Developing a comprehensive divergence trading plan involves setting clear criteria for entries and exits. For bullish divergences, you might decide to enter a trade once the price breaks above a specific resistance level following the divergence. Conversely, for bearish divergences, you might short the asset when it breaks below a support level. Establishing these rules beforehand can assist in maintaining discipline and consistency, crucial traits for successful trading.

Let's delve into an example to see divergence trading in action. Suppose you're analyzing the EUR/USD pair and you spot a bullish divergence on the daily chart. You've noticed that while the price is making lower lows, the MACD histogram is making higher lows, indicating a weakening bearish momentum. You decide to corroborate this signal on the 4-hour chart, finding a similar divergence. Your entry strategy could involve waiting for the price to close above a recent resistance level. Meanwhile, your stop loss is strategically placed below the recent swing low, protecting you against a false breakout.

On the flip side, imagine you're observing the GBP/USD pair and detect a bearish divergence. The price charts show higher highs, yet the RSI is slipping lower, indicating diminishing bullish momentum. After verifying this signal on a shorter timeframe, perhaps the 1-hour chart, you prepare to short the pair as it breaches a key support level. Setting your stop loss above the recent high helps to mitigate risk if the divergence fails.

It's vital to note the importance of patience and timing in divergence trading. Jumping into trades prematurely or hesitating to exit can lead to missed opportunities or unnecessary losses. Mastering the art of divergence trading requires consistent practice, continuous learning, and adapting to ever-changing market conditions.

In conclusion, trading bullish and bearish divergences involves more than recognizing when they occur. It's about confirming signals across multiple timeframes, utilizing a confluence of other technical analysis tools, implementing robust risk management strategies, and adhering to a disciplined trading plan. With these elements in place, you can make divergence trading a potent component of your trading arsenal, enhancing your ability to spot trend reversals and capitalize on them effectively.

Combining Divergences with Other Strategies

Forex trading is an intricate dance requiring precise moves and sharp attention to numerous factors. Divergence trading, a strategy where price and indicator movements diverge, offers powerful insights into potential market reversals. But mastering divergence trading doesn't happen in isolation. To achieve peak efficiency and consistency, traders should blend divergences with other strategies. Doing so not only fortifies their market approach but also enhances their odds of success.

Start with a well-rounded understanding of technical analysis essentials. For instance, combining divergences with support and resistance levels can be a game-changer. When price action shows a divergence near a key support or resistance zone, it often signifies a more robust market reversal. Imagine spotting a bullish divergence when the price reaches a significant support level—an excellent setup for a long trade. This integration strengthens the signal, reducing the noise and false alarms that come from relying on divergences alone.

Volume and momentum indicators also play a crucial part in this strategy blend. The Moving Average Convergence Divergence (MACD) and the Relative Strength Index (RSI) are particularly effective. When these indicators align with a divergence, they offer additional layers of validation. For example, in bearish markets, a bearish divergence combined with decreasing volume can add weight to the bearish sentiment, convincing traders to short the asset or tighten their stop loss. Conversely, in bullish markets, a bullish divergence with increasing volume can confirm the uptrend and encourage traders to hold their positions longer.

Price action strategies themselves, without dependency on indicators, are another vital element to combine with divergences. Pin bars and engulfing patterns, for example, when identified alongside divergence signals, can offer enhanced confirmation for trade entries. If a trader notices a bearish divergence followed by a bearish engulfing pattern, it often points to a significant market downturn. This redundancy across different methods generally reassures traders, giving them the confidence to execute their strategies more reliably.

Risk management, integral to any robust trading system, finds better enforcement when we include divergence strategies. Position sizing, stop loss, and take-profit levels can be fine-tuned using divergences. Suppose a trader encounters a bullish divergence but is uncertain about the extent of the price move. By adjusting the stop loss to just below the support level and locking in profits at predetermined levels, traders minimize risks and ensure profits, even if the market reverses sooner than expected.

While trading divergences, employing algorithmic strategies can also offer substantial advantages. Automated systems can scan markets perpetually, identifying divergences and other confirming signals, often faster than the human eye. Backtesting such systems with historical data helps refine strategies and validates their robustness. Traders can incorporate algorithms to manage the intricacies of divergence trading while mitigating emotional decision-making biases.

It's also wise not to overlook fundamental analysis when blending divergences with other strategies. Economic indicators like GDP growth rates, employment data, or central bank announcements often provide additional context. If a bearish divergence in a currency pair coincides with weak employment data, traders have a robust basis for a short position. Coupling divergences with fundamental factors enriches traders' perspectives and allows for more informed decisions, reducing the reliance on technical indicators alone.

Incorporation of these diverse elements creates a layered, multi-faceted approach to trading divergences. It's like weaving a safety net: even if one strand frays, several others hold firm, maintaining the overall integrity of your strategy. This multi-layering tactic not only brings clarity but also significantly enhances the effectiveness of trade setups, providing more actionable insights and higher probability trades.

Remember, however, that no strategy is infallible on its own. Diversifying approaches ensures traders aren't left vulnerable should one method underperform. Combining divergences with other strategies fosters a cartel of sorts, where each method backs up the others, ultimately increasing resilience and trading longevity.

Let's delve further into a practical example. Consider a scenario where you've identified a bearish divergence on a daily chart of the EUR/USD pair. The RSI indicates overbought conditions, and you've spotted an ascending trendline acting as a resistance level. What if the upcoming economic calendar announces a significant market-moving event like an ECB meeting? By layering this fundamental analysis over your existing divergence and technical signals, you've created a multifaceted decision-making structure. The collective validation heightens the trade's potential success, prepared to capitalize on the market's reaction.

Incorporating diverse elements also assists in refining exit strategies. For example, if your initial divergence trade has hit a partial profit target but is meeting robust resistance while your other indicators warn of an impending reversal, it might be prudent to exit the trade entirely or tighten your stops. This foresight, developed through a composite strategy, ensures capital preservation and profit maximization.

By integrating these elements, traders can adapt to the ever-changing landscape of Forex markets. Divergences, while powerful, serve as pieces of a broader puzzle. When paired with other strategies, they not only paint more comprehensive market pictures but also guide traders toward more judicious, data-driven decisions. The ultimate goal is to be dynamic and strategic, constantly iterating on approaches to stay ahead of market movements.

To conclude, the amalgamation of divergence trading with other strategies forms a cohesive, well-rounded trading approach. This synergy leverages multiple market perspectives, ensuring that no single point of failure can undermine an entire strategy. For intermediate to advanced traders aiming for heightened efficiency and profitability, this multifaceted method stands as an indispensable pillar. Embrace it, refine it, and watch your trading acumen soar to new heights.

Chapter 12: The Global Impact on Forex Trading

In today's interconnected world, understanding the global impact on Forex trading is paramount for intermediate and advanced traders aiming to refine their strategies. Geopolitical events can swiftly influence currency valuations, and keeping an eye on international news can give traders an edge. Currency correlations add another layer of complexity, requiring a nuanced understanding of how different currency pairs move in relation to one another. Additionally, emerging markets bring unique challenges and opportunities, as their economic shifts can have cascading effects on established currencies. Mastery of these global influences allows traders to make more informed decisions, ultimately enhancing their profitability and trading acumen.

The Effect of Geopolitical Events

Geopolitical events can be game-changers in the Forex market. A single political decision or diplomatic incident can send currency prices soaring or plunging. These events encompass everything from elections and referendums to international treaties and conflicts. Understanding their impact isn't just beneficial—it's crucial for any trader looking to navigate the intricate web of currency movements effectively.

One stark example is Brexit, which caused substantial volatility in the Forex market. The UK's decision to leave the European Union immediately impacted the British Pound. Traders who kept a close eye on the unfolding political drama were able to capitalize on the fluctuations. This event demonstrated how political uncertainty could lead to significant trading opportunities and risks. Anticipating or reacting promptly to such events is where advanced traders can truly leverage their expertise.

Election cycles also play a significant role. Political campaigns, debates, and the eventual election of new leaders bring a sense of uncertainty. This uncertainty can lead to short-term volatility as traders speculate on how the new administration's policies will affect the economy. For example, U.S. presidential elections often create ripples across global markets, influencing not just the US Dollar but also other major currencies due to the global interconnectedness of economies.

Geopolitical tensions, especially involving major economies, can drastically affect Forex trading. Consider the trade wars between the U.S. and China. Tariffs and retaliatory measures between these two economic giants caused widespread fluctuation in currency valuations. Traders who could interpret policy changes and predict the economic fallout were better positioned to make profitable trades amidst the chaos.

International sanctions represent another crucial element. When a country faces sanctions, its economy and currency often suffer. An excellent case in point is Iran. Imposed sanctions led to a devaluation of the Iranian Rial and created ripple effects for other currencies in the region. Knowing how to navigate such politically induced market movements can equip traders with the ability to make informed decisions that significantly affect their bottom line.

Similarly, geopolitical stability acts as a stabilizing factor for currencies. Nations with stable governments and predictable policies often see their currencies perform more reliably. Forex traders frequently prefer dealing in currencies where geopolitical risks are lower, interpreting stability as a sign of economic strength.

Wars and conflicts undeniably disrupt Forex markets. The uncertainty and fear associated with these events can lead to risk aversion, with traders flocking to safe-haven currencies like the US Dollar, Swiss Franc, or Japanese Yen. Monitoring news headlines for the latest developments is crucial for traders aiming to avoid potential pitfalls or capitalize on arising opportunities.

It's also vital to understand the interconnected nature of global politics. An event in one country can have a domino effect on multiple currencies. For instance, political turmoil in an emerging market can lead to a devaluation of its currency, which may then impact related currencies or trading partners. Forex traders must, therefore, adopt a comprehensive perspective, considering not just isolated events but broader geopolitical trends.

Policy shifts in organizations like the European Union can also affect currency markets. When the EU implements new regulations or economic measures, the Euro and related currencies often respond almost immediately. For instance, the European Central Bank's monetary policies can have far-reaching effects that traders need to analyze and incorporate into their trading strategies.

Geopolitical risk isn't just about large-scale events. Smaller, localized issues can also impact Forex trading. Political scandals, sudden policy changes, or even notable speeches by influential leaders can create market tremors. For example, a significant speech by the Federal Reserve Chair on monetary policy can immediately influence the US Dollar's value.

Seasoned Forex traders keep a keen eye on geopolitical developments through news outlets, governmental announcements, and specialized geopolitical analysis. Having real-time information allows traders to make quick, informed decisions. They leverage financial news services, social media, and analytical tools to stay ahead of the curve. The goal is to anticipate market movements rather than just react to them.

Utilizing geopolitical analysis tools and subscribing to geopolitical risk assessments from reputable agencies can give traders an edge. These resources offer in-depth insights and forecasts, making it easier to strategize and adapt trading plans. Incorporating this data into a comprehensive trading plan enables more robust risk management and better decision-making.

Ultimately, understanding the impact of geopolitical events on Forex trading is about connecting the dots. It's about seeing how political dynamics drive economic policies and, consequently, currency values. By integrating geopolitical awareness into their analytical toolkit, traders can better navigate market volatility and identify profitable opportunities amid global upheavals.

Adopting a strategic and informed approach to geopolitical events can turn potential risks into opportunities. By being proactive and continuously updating their knowledge base, intermediate and advanced Forex traders can stay ahead in an ever-changing landscape. This practice not only enhances profitability but also cultivates a deeper comprehension of the intricate connections between global politics and currency markets.

Currency Correlations and Forex

Currency correlations are a critical aspect of Forex trading that can significantly impact a trader's decision-making process. Understanding how different currency pairs are interconnected allows traders to manage their portfolios more effectively, optimize their risk management strategies, and capitalize on market opportunities that would otherwise be overlooked.

A currency correlation refers to the relationship between two currency pairs and how they move in relation to one another. These correlations can be positive, negative, or neutral, indicating whether the pairs move together, move inversely, or show no discernible pattern respectively. Positive correlations mean that as one currency pair rises, the other pair also tends to rise. For example, EUR/USD and GBP/USD often show positive correlations because both pairs are typically quoted against the US dollar. On the contrary, negative correlations imply that when one currency pair increases, the other decreases. A classic example of this would be EUR/USD and USD/CHF, since they tend to move in opposite directions.

To make the most of currency correlations, traders should incorporate them into their strategies. Correlations can provide insights into diversification and risk management by avoiding simultaneous trades in highly correlated pairs. For instance, if you're already holding a long position in EUR/USD, taking an additional long position in GBP/USD might inadvertently double your exposure to the same market movements. Conversely, understanding these relationships can also uncover arbitrage opportunities or hedge positions more effectively.

One essential tool for evaluating currency correlations is the correlation matrix. This matrix offers a quantitative view of how different currency pairs are related over specific periods. Data points are presented in the form of correlation coefficients, ranging from -1 to 1. A coefficient of +1 indicates a perfect positive correlation, -1 indicates a perfect negative correlation, and a value near 0 suggests no correlation. By examining these values, traders can make calculated decisions regarding their trades, balancing their portfolios and mitigating unnecessary risks.

It's important to note that correlations aren't static; they can and do change over time. A pair that is positively correlated today might not exhibit the same behavior tomorrow due to various factors, such as changes in economic policies, geopolitical events, or market sentiment shifts. Hence, maintaining current and historical correlation data is paramount for ongoing strategy refinement.

Geopolitical events often play a substantial role in altering currency correlations. Trade agreements, political instability, or economic sanctions can shift how currencies interact with each other. For example, Brexit had a significant impact on the correlation between EUR/USD and GBP/USD, causing the previously strong positive correlation to weaken. Traders must stay updated on these events to adapt their strategies in real-time, ensuring that their risk management remains robust despite rapidly changing conditions.

Moreover, central bank policies can greatly influence currency correlations. Monetary policy decisions, such as interest rate changes or quantitative easing programs, can impact currency strength and correlations. For instance, if the US Federal Reserve decides to raise interest rates, the USD may strengthen, affecting its correlation with other currencies like EUR, GBP, and JPY. Traders must keep a close eye on economic calendars and central bank announcements, as these can provide foresight into potential correlation shifts.

Technology and data analysis tools play a crucial role in monitoring and interpreting currency correlations. Advanced platforms and analytics software can automate the calculation of correlation coefficients and provide visual representations of correlation changes over time. These tools can help traders quickly spot trends and anomalies, enabling them to make informed decisions backed by data.

While a clear understanding of currency correlations can be advantageous, it also requires a degree of caution. Over-reliance on fixed correlations can lead to misjudgments, as market conditions are continually evolving. Traders should use correlations as one of many tools in their analytical toolkit, and continuously verify their assumptions with updated market data.

Furthermore, correlations don't always hold during periods of high volatility or market crises. In such times, traditional correlation patterns might break down, requiring traders to rely more on their knowledge and understanding of market fundamentals and less on historical patterns. This underscores the necessity of staying adaptable and having contingency plans in place for unexpected market behavior.

To integrate currency correlations effectively into your trading plan, start by defining your risk tolerance and trading goals. From there, analyze historical correlation data and continuously monitor current correlations. Aim to diversify your trades to reduce exposure to highly correlated pairs, and use hedging strategies where appropriate to safeguard your positions during market fluctuations.

In conclusion, understanding and utilizing currency correlations can enhance your Forex trading strategy, optimize your portfolio, and improve risk management. While dynamic and sometimes unpredictable, these correlations offer critical insights that can lead to more profitable trading decisions. Staying informed, adaptable, and data-driven will ensure you can leverage these correlations to your advantage, navigating the complexities of the Forex market with greater confidence and competence.

Emerging Markets and Their Influence

Emerging markets are increasingly becoming pivotal players in the global forex trading landscape. These economies, characterized by rapid industrialization and economic growth, significantly influence currency values and trading decisions. For intermediate and advanced Forex traders, understanding how emerging markets impact forex can provide a competitive edge.

It's essential to grasp the basic framework of what constitutes an emerging market. These are typically nations transitioning from low-income to middle-income status through economic reforms, increased productivity, and enhanced financial systems. Countries like Brazil, Russia, India, China, and South Africa—collectively known as the BRICS nations—are notable examples. Their rapid growth rates, compared to developed economies, can lead to greater volatility in their currencies, offering both opportunities and risks to Forex traders.

The volatility in emerging market currencies often stems from political instability, changes in government policies, and economic fluctuations. For instance, sudden governmental policy shifts in Brazil or geopolitical tensions in Russia can rapidly alter investor sentiment, causing significant swings in currency values. Understanding these dynamics enables traders to anticipate and react to potential market movements, enhancing their strategy and potentially increasing profitability.

Moreover, emerging markets are rich in natural resources, which play a critical role in their economic landscapes. Countries like Brazil and Russia are major exporters of commodities like oil and minerals. Consequently, their currencies are closely tied to the global commodity market's health. For forex traders, monitoring commodity prices alongside traditional economic indicators becomes crucial when dealing with emerging market currencies.

Additionally, the monetary policies of emerging markets are often more fluid and less predictable than those of developed nations. Central banks in these countries may adopt aggressive measures to control inflation, stabilize their currencies, or spur economic growth. For example, the People's Bank of China has a history of intervening heavily in the currency market to manage the yuan's value. Such interventions can lead to sudden, sharp movements in exchange rates, presenting both challenges and opportunities for astute traders.

The influence of emerging markets on forex trading is also seen through their integration into the global financial system. As these economies become more connected to global trade networks, their currencies experience increased liquidity and participation in the forex market. This integration often results in a more dynamic trading environment where trends and price movements can be more pronounced.

For many advanced forex traders, the allure of emerging markets lies in their growth potential. A growing economy typically sees increased foreign investment, leading to appreciation of its currency. However, this potential is coupled with risks such as political instability or sudden economic downturns. Therefore, a robust understanding of risk management is essential when operating in these markets. Techniques like stop-loss orders and position sizing become even more critical to safeguard against unforeseen market drops.

Another layer of complexity is introduced by the role of external influences on emerging markets. Factors such as global interest rates, trade policies, and international capital flows can profoundly affect these economies. For example, an interest rate hike by the U.S. Federal Reserve might result in capital outflows from emerging markets, leading to depreciation of their currencies. An adept trader must consider these external factors when devising strategies involving emerging market currencies.

Advanced traders often utilize a combination of technical and fundamental analysis to decode the complexities of emerging markets. Technical tools like moving averages and relative strength indices (RSIs) can be invaluable for identifying trends and potential entry or exit points. Fundamental analysis, on the other hand, involves scrutinizing economic indicators, political developments, and market sentiment to gauge a currency's future direction. By blending these approaches, traders can achieve a holistic view of emerging market dynamics.

One practical example is the relationship between the Chinese yuan and global manufacturing indices. By tracking data such as the Purchasing Managers' Index (PMI), traders can gain insights into China's manufacturing health, which directly influences the yuan's value. A rising PMI indicates expanding manufacturing activity, often leading to yuan appreciation, while a declining PMI suggests contraction, potentially causing depreciation. Such data-driven insights are invaluable for crafting informed trading strategies.

Similarly, the South African rand is influenced by the global gold market, given South Africa's role as a significant gold producer. Traders who keep a close eye on gold price trends can anticipate movements in the rand, adjusting their positions accordingly. This interconnectedness highlights the importance of a multi-faceted analytical approach when dealing with emerging market currencies.

Moreover, technological advancements and accessibility have made it easier for traders to participate in emerging market forex trading. The proliferation of online trading platforms and real-time data feeds allows traders to monitor and respond to market movements swiftly. This technological edge can be particularly advantageous in the fast-paced world of forex trading, where timing is often critical.

Understanding the transformative impact of emerging markets on the forex landscape is indispensable for sophisticated traders. These markets offer a unique blend of high growth potential and increased volatility, creating a dynamic trading environment. By integrating technical and fundamental analysis, managing risk prudently, and staying attuned to both local and global factors, traders can navigate the complexities of emerging markets and leverage their influence to enhance their trading performance.

In summary, emerging markets encapsulate a realm of potential within the forex trading world. Their influence is far-reaching and multifaceted, presenting a spectrum of opportunities and challenges.

Advanced and intermediate traders who comprehend these markets' nuances stand to benefit from their dynamic nature. By combining robust analytical tools, strategic risk management, and a keen understanding of both local and international events, traders can effectively harness the power of emerging markets to advance their forex trading endeavors.

This Book Review Request

If you've delved into the nuanced realms of geopolitical events, currency correlations, and the influence of emerging markets as detailed in previous sections, we ask that you share your thoughts and experiences with this book to benefit fellow traders aiming to expand their expertise in the dynamic Forex market.

Conclusion

In wrapping up this comprehensive guide, it's essential to recognize that mastering Forex trading is not about quick fixes or shortcuts. It demands a nuanced understanding of the market, a careful selection and application of strategies, and a relentless focus on continual education and self-improvement. Through refining your technical analysis skills, effectively using indicators, managing risk prudently, and cultivating the right trading psychology, you're well on your way to enhancing your trading proficiency and profitability. Each chapter has equipped you with the tools and insights needed to navigate the complexities of Forex trading. As you integrate these sophisticated techniques and strategies into your trading regimen, remember that consistency and discipline are your greatest allies. Your journey as an intermediate to advanced Forex trader is just beginning, and the path ahead is filled with exciting opportunities for growth and success.

Appendix A: Appendix

The Appendix is intended to be your go-to reference for essential Forex trading resources that will bolster your journey towards becoming a more proficient and profitable trader. Below, we've organized key sources and tools that can provide valuable insights, performance tracking, and market analysis.

1. Forex Trading Resources

We've gathered a list of indispensable resources that every intermediate to advanced Forex trader should consider incorporating into their toolbox. These resources range from educational sites and analytical tools to forums and software, each capable of providing the support you need to refine your trading strategies.

1. Educational Websites and Courses:

These platforms offer comprehensive courses and articles on both basic and advanced Forex trading concepts.

- *BabyPips:* Known for its user-friendly guides and in-depth courses that cover Forex from the ground up, BabyPips is an essential resource for continuous learning.
- *Court;* An effective platform for advanced traders looking to refine their strategies through specialized courses and webinars.

2. Market Analysis Tools:

Stay ahead of the game with these indispensable tools that offer real-time market data and sophisticated charting capabilities.

- *MetaTrader 4/5:* Offering a comprehensive suite of charting tools, technical indicators, and automated trading options, this is a must-have for serious traders.
- *TradingView:* Known for its powerful charting capabilities and community-driven ideas, it's an excellent tool for technical analysis.

3. News Sources and Economic Calendars:

Stay informed on global economic events that influence market conditions.

- *Forex Factory:* A robust platform offering up-to-the-minute news, economic calendars, and forums for trader discussions.
- *Investing.com:* Offers comprehensive news coverage, real-time data, and in-depth market analysis.

4. Community and Forums:

Engage with other traders to exchange ideas, strategies, and insights.

- *Elite Trader:* A forum where professional traders share their strategies and experiences.
- *ForexPeaceArmy:* This forum is great for reviews on brokers, as well as strategy discussions and alerts on potential scams.

5. Performance Tracking and Journaling:

Tools and platforms to help you maintain records of your trades and analyze performance.

- *Myfxbook:* A robust platform for tracking your trading performance, analyzing your trades, and sharing results with the community.

- *Trading Journal Spreadsheet:* Simple, customizable spreadsheets that allow you to log every trade and sift through data to identify patterns and assess progress.

Utilizing these resources can make a significant difference in your trading journey. The key is not just to access them but to integrate them into your everyday trading routine to consistently improve and adapt.

Armed with these resources, you're better prepared to tackle the ever-evolving Forex market landscape and make informed, strategic trading decisions that enhance your overall performance and profitability.

Forex Trading Resources

As you dive deeper into the world of Forex trading, having the right resources at your fingertips can make a significant difference in your success. This section will walk you through some of the most essential tools, platforms, and educational materials available to enhance your trading journey.

Let's start with **educational websites and forums**. Numerous websites offer a treasure trove of information ranging from basic principles to advanced strategies. Sites like Investopedia, BabyPips, and FXStreet provide a wide array of articles, tutorials, and news updates that can help enhance your understanding of various trading concepts. Moreover, forums such as Forex Factory and TradingView allow traders to share insights, strategies, and experiences. Engaging in these communities can give you valuable perspectives and tips from fellow traders who share similar goals and challenges.

In addition to websites, **books and eBooks** are indispensable resources for an in-depth understanding of Forex trading. Classics such as "Currency Trading for Dummies" by Brian Dolan and "The Little Book of Currency Trading" by Kathy Lien offer excellent introductions and cover fundamental and technical strategies comprehensively. For those who prefer digital formats, eBooks and audiobooks can be convenient options, allowing you to absorb knowledge on the go.

On the technical front, accessing high-quality **charting and analysis tools** is crucial. MetaTrader 4 (MT4) and MetaTrader 5 (MT5) are among the most widely used trading platforms offering robust charting capabilities, a wide array of indicators, and the ability to automate trading using Expert Advisors (EAs). TradingView is another exceptional platform that provides comprehensive charting tools and allows traders to share and follow trading ideas.

For staying updated with the latest market news and economic data, subscribing to **financial news services** can be immensely beneficial. Bloomberg, Reuters, and CNBC offer real-time news updates and analysis. Moreover, economic calendars like those found on Investing.com or Forex Factory can help traders keep track of major economic events and announcements that could affect the Forex markets.

When it comes to risk management, having access to **risk assessment tools** can make all the difference. Calculators for position sizing, pip value, and risk-to-reward ratios are available on various trading websites. These tools can help ensure you are managing your capital effectively and making informed decisions about your trades.

Beyond online resources, **broker services** play a pivotal role in the trading experience. Selecting a reliable broker with low spreads, fast execution, and excellent customer service is vital. Many brokers offer demo accounts, which enable traders to practice their strategies in a simulated trading environment without risking real money. Popular brokers like OANDA, FXCM, and IG provide robust platforms and comprehensive resources to assist traders of all experience levels.

Considering the fast-paced nature of Forex trading, having the right **mobility tools** can enhance your ability to monitor and react to market movements. Mobile trading apps available on iOS and Android platforms ensure that you can keep an eye on your portfolio and execute trades no matter where you are. Apps like MetaTrader and cTrader are highly regarded for their user-friendly interfaces and powerful functionalities.

Another potent resource is **algorithmic trading software**. For those who venture into automated trading, software like MetaTrader's Expert Advisors, NinjaTrader, and ZuluTrade offer opportunities to develop, test, and deploy trading algorithms. These platforms often come with backtesting capabilities, allowing you to assess the performance of your strategies against historical data before committing real capital.

To ensure continuous improvement and adapt to evolving market conditions, participating in **online courses** and webinars can be highly advantageous. Websites like Udemy, Coursera, and the Online Trading Academy offer courses on various aspects of Forex trading, from beginner to advanced levels. Webinars hosted by seasoned traders or financial experts provide real-time insights and allow for interactive learning experiences.

Lastly, subscribing to **trading journals and analysis reports** can provide ongoing learning and reflection. Keeping a trading journal helps track your trades, emotions, and outcomes, leading to valuable self-analysis and improvement. Various apps and software like Edgewonk and Tradervue can streamline this process, making it easier to log and analyze your trades. Meanwhile, subscribing to analysis reports from reputable financial institutions can give you broader market perspectives and strategies to consider.

To sum up, leveraging a diverse array of resources is key to staying informed, developing robust strategies, and maintaining a competitive edge in Forex trading. The right combination of educational materials, technical tools, broker services, mobility solutions, and continuous learning platforms can significantly enhance your trading prowess and profitability.

Glossary of Key Terms

This glossary provides definitions and explanations of essential Forex trading terms. These terms are fundamental to understanding the intricacies of the Forex market and enhancing trading strategies.

- **Ask Price:** The price at which a trader can buy a currency pair. It is also known as the offer price and is typically higher than the bid price.
- **Bid Price:** The price at which a trader can sell a currency pair. The bid price is usually lower than the ask price.
- **Broker:** An intermediary who executes trades on behalf of retail traders and institutions in the Forex market.
- **Bull Market:** A market condition where prices are rising, encouraging buying.
- **Bear Market:** A market condition where prices are falling, encouraging selling.
- **Candlestick Chart:** A type of financial chart that displays the high, low, open, and close prices of a security for a specific period.
- **Currency Pair:** The quotation of two different currencies, with the value of one currency being quoted against the other. For example, EUR/USD.

- **Drawdown:** The peak-to-trough decline during a specific period for an investment, trading account, or fund.
- **Economic Indicator:** A statistical measure that reflects the economic condition of a country, influencing currency value and Forex trading decisions.
- **Exchange Rate:** The value at which one currency can be exchanged for another currency.
- **Fibonacci Retracement:** A method of technical analysis for determining support and resistance levels by identifying key points of retracement on a price chart.
- **Leverage:** The use of borrowed capital to increase the potential return of an investment. In Forex, it allows traders to control larger positions with a smaller amount of capital.
- **Lot:** A standardized quantity of a financial instrument in trading. In Forex, a standard lot typically represents 100,000 units of the base currency.
- **Margin:** The amount of money required to open a leveraged trading position. It is a fraction of the total trade size.
- **Pip:** The smallest price movement in the Forex market, typically equal to 0.0001 for most currency pairs.
- **Spread:** The difference between the bid and ask price of a currency pair. It represents the broker's profit.
- **Stop Loss:** An order to sell a security when it reaches a certain price, limiting a trader's loss on a position.
- **Take Profit:** An order to sell a security when it reaches a certain price, securing a trader's profit on a position.

- **Volatility:** A statistical measure of the dispersion of returns for a given security or market index. Higher volatility indicates higher price swings.

This glossary encapsulates key terms crucial for Forex traders aiming to deepen their market understanding, refine their strategies, and optimize their trading outcomes.

www.ingramcontent.com/pod-product-compliance
Lightning Source LLC
LaVergne TN
LVHW100321210926
848480LV00003B/1210
* 9 7 8 1 9 2 3 4 5 2 2 5 1 *